WILL THE FINAL GENERATION PLEASE STAND ?

Understanding Christian Identity and Journeying with Jesus

LORRAINE PATIENCE

VESSELS OF VIRTUES

Published by Vessels of Virtues Publishers
A unit of Vessels of Virtues Ministries Lancaster,
United Kingdom
admin@vesselsofvirtues.com
www.vesselsofvirtues.com

 Unless otherwise indicated, Scripture quotations are taken from the New International Version (NIV) of the Holy Bible.

ISBN: 978-1-8381554-4-5

Designed by Vessels of Virtues Publishers and printed in Great Britain.

Printed in Great Britain by Bell and Bain Ltd, Glasgow

Content

Dedication

I would like to dedicate this book firstly to Jesus who is the author and finisher of my faith. I give You all the glory Jesus, without You I would never have put pen to paper. Thank you for inviting me to 'Enter In' and for entrusting me with the things that You have placed deep within my heart. There is no greater privilege than living my life for You, I am eternally thankful.

Secondly, to my very dear friend Mary Ratcliff who has gone home to be with the Lord, now safe and secure in His arms. She was an amazing prayer warrior full of faith and she taught me so much. I'm sorry she never had the chance to read my book, I know she would have been proud of me.

Finally, to all those who read this book with a hungry heart for more of Jesus. I pray that within these pages you will find some encouragement which will propel you forward and that you will 'Enter In' to all that He has for you in these 'end-of-the-end days.'

Acknowledgements

I would like to thank my wonderful husband, Ali, who has always supported me and encouraged me in every endeavour, always by my side cheering me on. Also, my children Beccy, Alex and Matthew. Thank you.

I would like to thank Dr. Ayodele Afuye and his wife Tomi, along with all the team at Vessels of Virtue Publishing, for making this book a reality, for believing in me and encouraging me to finish it.

To very dear friends Roger and Glenys London. Roger's teaching has shaped and moulded me significantly over these last 10 years. So many things that I had known in my spirit fell into place when I met this wonderful couple.

Thank you to my dear friends Linda Robinson and Carole Clayton, for all their encouragement. Carole, thank you for the many hours you sat with me in front of the computer screen editing.

It would be impossible to thank everyone who has played a part in this work. Over the years there have been many people who have inputted into my life and my Christian journey, moulding me and shaping me along the way. Thank you all for your help and encouragement but, most of all, for believing in me. Mum and Dad - Barry and Marlene Smith, Ron and Christine Farrington, Pete and Rhian Goulding, Carol Halton, Ray and Anne Robertson, Zachariah Ken Fullah. Thank you all for your love, encouragement, and support over the years.

Endorsements

"Lorraine has written a message of intimacy with God, and with precision, created a picture of "doing it the way it should be done" with Christ as the greatest example. Believers who are serious, and really want to experience the expected growth in their journey with Jesus would appreciate the book, as it would be a great resource to them".

Dr. Ayodele Afuye. DMin. MSc. BA. (Hons)
Senior Leader, Vessels of Virtues Ministries UK

"It has been my pleasure to edit this book. Lorraine writes candidly and with passion. She shares from her own revelation and balances this carefully with scripture".

Carole Clayton
Gateway House Church, Morecambe UK

Lorraine Patience writes with passion and conviction about how important it is that we find our true identity in Christ. As we seek deeper purity and consecration to do His will in these very late end times, God will use us to bless others and extend His Kingdom. There is little time before Jesus returns! This is a very inspirational and exhortative book and bang on theologically. It will encourage you to seek Jesus even more earnestly. Do take her message seriously!

Christopher Eve *BSc (Hons), MA*
The Dynasty Church, Lancaster, UK

The book's title expresses the view that this final generation of Christian believers need to stand up and be counted like never before. Lorraine deals with issues of the heart that are often overlooked or minimised by many believers, on the need to live practical but holy lives, lives that are daily being transformed into the likeness of Jesus.

Roger London
(UK Director of Transformed International)

Foreword

In this book you will encounter the Lorraine that my wife, Glenys, and I have grown to love and value since our first meeting at the Grapevine Christian Camp a decade or so ago. Lorraine is a straightforward Christian woman, who is absolutely passionate for Jesus and His Kingdom. Many who read this book will easily relate with Lorraine's down-to earth 'telling it like it is' approach. Her Christian testimony, outlined in the book in several of the chapters, is one of those 'ordinary' ones (is any testimony really ordinary?) that many will relate to and be compelled to keep reading, in order to discover how this Morecambe wife and mother has grown so much in her relationship and walk with Jesus. Lorraine doesn't mince her words, but all her words have been personally owned and put into practice over many years. Lorraine's practical instructions on how to go deeper and higher with God will resonate with many, who have a longing for more of God, but, perhaps, have never quite fulfilled their longing, for whatever reason.

The context for the book is a firm belief that we are, as Lorraine expresses it, in the 'end of the end days'. As she rightly states, these are days that will be challenging for every true disciple of Jesus, but ones where there will be the opportunity to experience the presence and power of God in an unprecedented way. The book's title expresses the view that this final generation of Christian believers need to stand up and be counted like never before. Lorraine deals with issues of the heart that are often overlooked or minimised by many believers, on the need to live practical but holy lives, lives that are daily being transformed into the likeness of Jesus.

Anyway, enjoy the read – I'm sure you will. But be ready to be challenged – I certainly was! Be inspired to follow in Lorraine's footsteps. Most importantly, press on, becoming more and more like Jesus, ready and waiting for His return.

Roger London (UK Director of Transformed International)

Introduction

This book is my response to promptings by Holy Spirit to write down the things I felt He was saying to me during the COVID-19 lockdown in 2020. Many of these things relate to the times we are now living in. I am not a theologian and don't see myself as an author, but I love Jesus, and I'm passionate about sharing His Word and the things He shows me. I have always hesitated to put pen to paper, feeling more comfortable sharing in person.

I wanted to write a book that was easy to understand, simple and straightforward, because I am a no-nonsense, straight-talking kind of person. I am, in many ways, a visionary and the Lord often speaks to me in pictures and reveals His purposes to me this way.

Much of what I write here, has been at the heart of my walk with the Lord over many years. The past few months I have been on an exciting journey that has led me to a place of new discovery in my walk with Him. This has given me fresh revelation that I believe I have been guided to share.

Who am I to do this, you may say? I've thought the same myself! However, I feel strongly that I am meant to follow the Lord's prompting by being obedient to share the things He has placed on my heart.

Over the years the Lord has spoken to me many times about the heart. The condition of our heart is key to our walk with Him. The Lord challenges us to search our hearts and to be honest about what we find there. We want to finish the race well, to be rewarded as good and faithful servants. I wonder if we truly understand how important this is for us in these days.

There is so much happening right now in the world that mirrors the warnings we see in the book of Revelation. We are facing the very real possibility that we could be the final generation of believers before Jesus returns for His Bride - the Church. God is calling us to a deeper level of faith in Him, a deeper level of intimacy. He is calling us to a place that many of us have resisted until now - a place of total surrender.

We need to die to our self. In order to do this, we must first understand who HE is and who we are in HIM. We need to recognise, acknowledge, and accept that all He says about us and who we are in Him is true. We need to believe that when He says we can 'do all things through Christ who strengthens us' - that we already have all that we need within us to accomplish 'all things'. We don't only need to understand these things, but we must also act upon them, accepting the commission that He calls all believers to. Faith without works is dead. It is time for us to stand up and enter in to all that He has for us in these days, all that has been purchased for us through Jesus' sacrifice on the cross. There is so much more than many of us have yet understood or experienced.

It is my heartfelt prayer that this book will awaken a desire in you to rise up and seek His face in a new way in these 'end-of-the-end days'; that your heart will be stirred by Holy Spirit into such a place of openness and clarity that you will no longer be distracted by the things of this world, by its passions and its pains; that you will be strengthened in your spirit to stand strong; that you will be unshakeable no matter what goes on around you. Time is short, there is no time to delay in answering His call.

It is a sad fact that not everyone who professes to be a believer will be saved. It is about our heart response to God - not merely our mind. So, we can think we are clear about our salvation, but Jesus tells us in Matthew Chapter 7:21-23,

> *"Not everyone who says to me, 'Lord, Lord,' will enter the kingdom of heaven, but only the one who does the will of my Father who is in heaven. Many will say to me on that day, 'Lord, Lord, did we not prophesy in your name and in your name drive out demons and, in*

> *your name, perform many miracles?' Then I will tell them plainly, 'I never knew you. Away from me, you evildoers!"*

1 Timothy 4:1 tells us that many will be deceived and fall away from the Lord.

> *"The Spirit clearly says that in later times some will abandon the faith and follow deceiving spirits and things taught by demons."*

It is my prayer that God will challenge us all in these days, and that we will be willing to be open to all that He has for us. Are we willing to change some of our foundational beliefs, if necessary? Are we willing to open our hearts to Him - to be laid bare before Him who already sees and knows us in the deepest parts of our souls? Will we lay our hearts on the altar of sacrifice, allowing God to reconstruct, repair, reshape, heal, and regenerate us, restoring our hearts into the original form and so transforming us into His image? The image of Christ.

If we are willing, then it is my belief that God will recalibrate us, taking us back to 'factory settings'. He will remove all the dross we have gathered over the years and refine us in the furnace of His Love. Are you willing to be broken so you can be remade anew? Prepare yourself for a huge outpouring of God's Holy Spirit if you are willing for this breaking. It is in the emptying of our self that we become vessels prepared for God's purposes. He is true to His promise. He will fill you when you are empty. Now is the time to get ready. God wants to use you in more ways than you can ever imagine. He wants to fulfil the dreams and visions He gave you in the past. He will reissue calls that you never answered, and you will live in the fullness of all He intended for you. John 10:10 says,

> *"The thief comes only to steal and kill and destroy; I have come that they may have life and have it to the full."*

Unfortunately, many Christians never experience the fullness of this life here on earth, often living defeated lives, struggling with self-doubt and unbelief. They never become the overcomers that we hear Jesus speak of in the Bible, the overcomers that He intended them to be. They do not live victorious lives in Christ Jesus. I am not saying I have always lived a full life, but I live a much fuller life than I did at first. I have learned how to be open and honest with myself and to lay my heart bare before God. I am trying to live an authentic life by allowing Him to deal with me on a day-to-day basis so that I can fully become the person He created me to be. I am trusting Him to complete this work in me. I still have a long way to go but I am on my way - walking daily with Him. Each day I pray I am more like Jesus than I was the previous day.

Over 20 years ago, around 1999, God gave me a picture of a heart being circumcised and over the years this picture has shaped my journey as a disciple of Jesus. I have been encouraged and challenged to be honest with myself, and honest with God. Even though God sees everything, He still desires that intimacy with me. He wants me to be honest with Him. He yearns for that open, honest, trusting relationship. I am becoming more transparent in my relationship with Him as time goes on.

Deuteronomy 30:6 says,

> *"The LORD your God will circumcise your hearts and the hearts of your descendants, so that you may love him with all your heart and with all your soul, and live."*

The greatest desire of my heart is to see believers becoming true disciples of Jesus, living lives laid down before Him in obedience to Holy Spirit. I pray in these last days that we will all increase in discernment and be able to stand strong in our faith without being deceived.

So, friends, are you ready? Will you open your heart to all that God has prepared for you? Will you make every moment count -

remembering that time is running out? Will you be an overcomer in this final generation? Will you stand and enter in to all that He has made available to you? I urge you to take some time to sit and pray, asking Holy Spirit to speak to you and to highlight all He wants to show you about the condition of your heart. May He touch you in the deepest part of your being as you allow yourself to become vulnerable before Him. He wants to heal and restore you and bring you into wholeness.

The remnant church is awakening and arising. Will you be amongst that number?

I am releasing a Spirit of Revelation and Truth

The Dream:

At the beginning of July 2021, I had a powerful dream. I was stood with a group of people who were gathered behind some metal railings. I was aware that they were protestors, and that we were all standing around what appeared to be a statue or monument. Alongside us there was another group of people who I believed to be local residents. My son was with me and he wanted to get involved with the protest, but I dissuaded him, not wanting him to get into trouble. I could see that many of the local residents were making phone calls and I assumed were ringing the police. Suddenly they began to move, gathering around the protestors, forming a protective wall. I realised they hadn't been calling the police at all. I told my son that I felt we were being protected and so it would now be safe to join with the protest group. Together with them we began peeling the outer layers off the monument to reveal what was underneath. These layers were made up of what appeared to be 'post it' notes that had completely covered it. I instantly knew they had been put there to hide the truth about what was hidden beneath. We were peeling off lies and deception in order to uncover the truth.

I saw another group coming towards us. They looked like security guards. Everyone had been trying to disperse, but the gate had been closed. As I walked towards it, the gate opened for me. I knew there was a key inside me that had caused it to open, and that I could use the key to both open and close the gate in the future. As I stood by the open gate, I awoke.

The Interpretation:

Over the next few weeks, I prayed about this dream, asking the Lord to reveal what He was trying to say to me. This is what I believe I heard from Him -

> *"I am releasing a spirit of revelation and truth, the peeling off of layers has begun! I am revealing secrets and laying bare the ugly truth. As we enter this new period of greater revelation, I am peeling off the layers of deception because the time has come for these outer layers that obscure the truth to be removed. The world has been deceived for far too long.*
>
> *Many of my saints have been deceived also, but I will no longer allow this. I am going to set free all who are truly searching for the truth in their hearts. Those who desire more of Me – those who want to go deeper and higher. I will set them free from the deception and lies that have imprisoned them for so long. I want them to fully know Me, so I am releasing them into the full truth, and that truth will set them free. They will finally know Me and understand who they are in Me.*
>
> *As I purify my saints and prepare them in this new era, I will use these newly purified ones to begin to peel off the layers of lies and deception to reveal truths previously hidden for generations. Those who are willing will be used of Me to reveal truth in these last days. These workers will be protected by Me in order to carry out this task. It will not be an easy assignment, they will be persecuted and attacked for standing against the world view, but if they continue to walk in obedience to this call - and if they trust me, I will protect them.*

These whom I have chosen for the task are currently in a purification process that will purge their hearts, burning up all that is not of My Spirit. When they are ready, they will be able to open doors that have been locked for generations, and these doors will be opened by the power of my Spirit working within them. Their obedience to the process is the key to this unlocking. I have given them power and authority to set captives free, to release those imprisoned within and to break chains of deception so that many will experience this freedom and run into My arms. Multitudes will be released before the worst deception of all time begins.

This revelation is twofold, firstly it exposes truth that has been hidden. The deception has been cleverly structured to appear safe and acceptable and easy to buy into, but my purified ones will bravely stand against it and go against the flow.

Secondly, these brave ones will assist others as they struggle in their escape from all the false truths that have controlled and manipulated them throughout their lives. They have been deceived into believing that all their hurts and all the pain they have experienced in the past has been totally cleansed from them, yet in reality they have the deep roots of these wounds still within, hindering them from moving forward in truth. Now is the time for the roots to be revealed and healed so that they can stand up and step out stronger and bolder, in service and ministry to others. Behold, I am doing a new thing! I am freeing them to live the full life that I intended. I want to reveal myself to the world through them.

These things will happen quickly - the healing process will be accelerated. My saints are beginning to realise that they are not yet whole, that many things they thought had been dealt with were never fully illuminated to be healed. This is a time of awakening to all that is locked deep within their souls. I am completing the work I began in them at the day of their salvation.

> *I will use them to reveal deceptions within my church, to help the deceived to unlearn some of the false structures that have been set in place. They will need a deep compassion for those who have walked in these false teachings as it will take the power of love without judgement to set them free. To those who are willing, I will release a spirit of revelation so that they will be enabled to embrace truth that was previously hidden from them, truth in an instant.*

BREAKOUT IS COMING - ***I am doing a new thing!"***

I believe this process has already begun. I am hearing testimonies from Christians who have experienced incredible, accelerated healing from years of pain that has been buried and locked inside. They thought they had dealt with it years ago through ministry and deliverance, but they had not been fully healed - the root remained. It had been partially healed and then the residue was locked away deep inside because it was just too painful to deal with at that time. I know from personal experience that God is moving in these days. Many things are changing in my life, I am changing, I am different. This renewing process is available to every believer. He wants to purify us. He wants us to be prepared, to be pure and Holy - set apart for His purposes. He wants us to be ready for the difficult days that lie ahead and ultimately for the return of Jesus, who is coming soon for His Bride.

I challenge you to take a look within. Where are you on this journey? Are you living the full life that Christ intended for you, or are you held back and struggling with pain from the past?

Jesus intended us to live the most abundant and fruitful life, a life of fullness and joy in Him. Is there something still missing for you? Have you been living a watered-down version of the Gospel, unable to overcome in some areas of life? It is possible there are some flaws in our theology that means we are not living as overcomers. Some of us may have inherited our theology from others without studying the scriptures for ourselves. Are we willing to ask Holy Spirit to correct us in the areas we may have got it wrong? He is revealing a spirit of revelation and of truth, are we ready to receive it and all that it may mean?

Wherever you are on your journey, ask the Lord to reveal Himself to you afresh. He wants us all to live totally free from the pressures of this world. Is now the time for you to break out of the mould - to live the abundant life He promised? It is time for you to live the full life that Jesus talks about in John 10:10:

> *"I have come that they might have life and life to the full"*

Let us check our hearts and ask God to show us where there are blockages that hinder us from living in freedom. Let us allow Holy Spirit to minister to us. Let us be honest with God and with ourselves. We should hold nothing back. We may need to cry, scream, shout and get on our knees, to make ourselves vulnerable before Him. We should do whatever it takes to come to that place of total surrender before Jesus. This will not be easy, but it will be worth it. It will be painful, and you may want to give up but press through. I believe it will be done quickly. I am reminded of the purifying of the temple. It says in 2 Chronicles 29:36,

> *"Hezekiah and all the people rejoiced at what God had brought about for his people, because it was done so quickly."*

God is speeding things up. Jesus is returning for His Bride very soon, and His Bride needs to be purified in preparation for Him. There is still much to do - we are not yet ready. There are also still many people across the globe who are not yet reached by the truth of the Gospel message. Time is short.

The time has come for us to breakout of the confinement that has restricted us for too long. It is time for the final generation to stand up and enter in to all that God has. We need to stand tall and strong and stand together in unity as His body here on the earth. Regardless of denomination or church background we are all ONE in Jesus. Where there is unity, the Lord commands a blessing. Can we dare to believe that The Church, The Body of Christ - The Bride - is finally awakening?

The bigger question is, are **YOU** among that number?

Returning to our First Love

In this chapter I want to suggest that you take a look back, and remember your first love, remember how you felt when you first met Jesus, when you first experienced a touch from Holy Spirit. Remember how much Jesus has already changed your life and how He loves you with an unconditional love. At times when you are feeling out of your comfort zone, when the Spirit of God is nudging you forward and it's uncomfortable to carry on reading, if you are feeling challenged, have confidence! You are not here by accident, there is something held within these pages that God wants to use to speak directly to you! He loves you more than you could ever imagine or comprehend, He wants to reveal more of Himself to you. I will begin by sharing my own story, the story of Jesus becoming my first love. It is neither dramatic nor full of signs and wonders, it is just an ordinary story of how Jesus has led and shaped my eternity, yet at the same time it is miraculous, as every true conversion is miraculous.

My Story

I was brought up in a Christian home and, as far back as I can remember, I have always gone to church. I remember visiting my nanna at her house and walking to the local park. I would be about seven years old at the time. There was a large tent in the park that day and someone invited me inside. I remember there was a man at the front talking about Jesus. He was quoting a scripture from Revelation 3:20:

> *"Here I am! I stand at the door and knock. If anyone hears my voice and opens the door, I will come in and eat with that person, and they with Me."*

The man then continued to invite people to open the door of their heart to Jesus. He said that it would be the best decision you could ever make. I can't remember much else, except that I felt compelled to move to the front of the tent. I accepted Jesus as my Saviour that day - and I never forgot that scripture, it was etched on my heart. It was the beginning of the most amazing journey, my life as a born-again believer.

As a child I was never one to use bad language, but one day in my final year of primary school I was in the playground with friends. I remember sensing a feeling of power - of actually being one of the 'big kids'. It was as though something suddenly clicked! I felt more powerful and began bossing some of the younger children and telling them what to do. I was running around the playground and as I moved to put my empty crisp packet in the bin the wind caught it and it blew away. For the first time in my life, I swore. It was as though a door had been opened in me and I began shouting and swearing. After that it became easier and easier to use bad language and be nasty to others. As I look back, I can vividly recall how that small incident in the school playground opened a door for the enemy to get into my life and how quickly it escalated into a bad habit. It is so easy to give the enemy a foothold in our lives, even from something so simple. We can often struggle to get back on track and so it is important to remember to keep short accounts, to always come to Jesus in repentance for even the smallest of things when we sense His prompting in our spirit. Don't let us forget that the enemy prowls around like a lion, ready to pounce on us in our moments of weakness.

In my first week at high school, I met a couple of new friends. I was acting tough to make myself feel big. As another girl came over and tried to join in with us, I called her a name and sent her away. I picked on the wrong girl that day, as a result of my actions she went on to make my life miserable throughout that first year of high school. I began being bullied by her and her friends and she turned the whole class against me. I used to call my mum, crying for her to come and take me home because I felt so awful. It was years later that the Lord reminded me of why this girl had turned on me in such a terrible way, He showed me how I had brought it all on myself.

I continued to attend church regularly with my parents. We were blessed to have a swimming pool in our garden which the church often used for baptismal services. As I sat watching one of these services and listening to the testimonies of those being baptised, the pastor asked if anyone else wanted to be baptised. I suddenly had an overwhelming desire to respond, I was eleven years old. I spoke with my pastor, and he was convinced of my understanding and so I was baptised that day. I was so excited, it was such an amazing experience and afterwards I remember feeling on top of the world.

In my teens I stopped attending church and lived life my own way. I had a long-term boyfriend, who ironically, happened to be the brother of the girl who had bullied me in the first year of high school. He wasn't a Christian and, as he wouldn't entertain the idea of going to church, I didn't go either. Occasionally I would attend with my parents and each time I would cry. I couldn't understand it then, but now I realise that God was drawing me back and convicting me through Holy Spirit.

At age twenty-two my relationship broke down and I decided to go back to church and recommit my life to Jesus. I began attending church regularly. In August 1989, I met my husband, Ali, and on our very first date I told him that I was a Christian. I was so surprised when he asked if he could come along with me to church, and we started attending church together. Despite my good intentions I moved in with Ali after only a few weeks of dating. We both continued to go to church every week and, after a few months, Ali gave his life to the Lord and became a Christian. I was thrilled, now I could live the Christian life I longed to live alongside my boyfriend the only problem being, we were living outside of God's will. We were going to church on Sundays, but we continued to live together as man and wife outside the commitment of marriage. One Sunday, a few weeks after Ali's conversion, I went to church alone as Ali was working at home removing a bathroom suite in our house. That Sunday the message was about the man who built his house on the sand. God spoke clearly to me, reminding me that I needed to build upon the rock. I felt so convicted that I moved back in with my parents the same day. I remember my cousin telling me that, if I honoured God, then God would honour me - and He did! Only a couple of days later Ali asked me to marry him. We had only been dating for six months but I knew he was the one for me and that God had brought us together for a purpose. We married four months later and we have never looked back.

Why am I telling you all this? It is because, despite the fact that I wandered away and gave the enemy a foothold in my life, I know that from the moment I accepted Jesus at the age of seven, He has never left my side. Even while I was going my own way, living my own selfish life, He never gave up on me. I suffered consequences due to my bad behaviour, but God used these as an illustration to show me how every action, however small, has a consequence.

Ali and I have had an amazing journey with Jesus. He has taken us on many adventures together over the past 30 plus years. Those adventures continue today. Jesus has been leading us the whole time. He is our rock, always there in times of trouble, and I have learned to rely on Him. Sometimes God allows me to go through times of pain and suffering yet I know I can trust Him, and that He is always causing all things to work together for my good, so that ultimately, I will be shaped and moulded into the very best version of myself. I can rest in the knowledge that He is in control. He knows what is needed to perfect me and will never allow me to be tested beyond my capacity to cope. He is my Jesus, my Saviour, my all. I love Him with all my life.

He can also be your all, if you allow Him. Can you trust Him in all things including the difficult times? In the pain and the struggles of your life? When nothing around you makes sense? When you feel lost and alone? Can you lean into Him, trusting Him daily with all your cares and concerns? He is working in you in order to perfect you. He will use the situations of your life to stretch you, mould you and shape you, strengthening you for what lies ahead. So don't resist Him, try not to fight against this perfecting of you. He is making you Holy, to be set apart for His purposes.

I was filled with Holy Spirit at the age of twenty-four, when on a lady's weekend away at a local Christian Retreat Centre. I fell under the power of the Holy Spirit along with three other ladies, and when we fell, we landed in the shape of a cross on the floor. It was an incredible experience. We all got up together and went out into the gardens laughing and screaming and dancing, feeling so alive and free. It felt as if nothing could hold us back anymore, we were so full of God. It was incredible.

Sometimes I look back and remind myself of this time, especially if I ever feel like giving up. I remind myself that God is the same yesterday, today and forever. He is always with me, just a prayer away. So, if you, like me, feel challenged at times by the working of Holy Spirit within, I encourage you to stop and reach out to God. When you have issues you don't want to deal with and maybe you don't feel ready to make the sacrifices necessary to be obedient to Him, reach out in prayer. Open your heart to Him. Remember the times when He has spoken in the past, when He has been so close that you could almost feel His breath on your cheek. Remember your first love, how you felt at the beginning and all He has done for you since. He has promised to lead you and protect you, to restore you and transform you. So don't give up! God will keep His promise to you. Now is the time for you to stand up and enter into all He has prepared for you in this final generation.

Who is our first love?

He is so much more than we can ever imagine. He is beyond all of our natural understanding. He is the one true God who lives in the three Divine persons of the Trinity. The Creator of the heavens and the earth. He is eternal, unchanging, unfathomable, holy and all powerful. He is love incarnate. He is full of compassion for the least and the lost; for the orphans and the widows; for you and for me. He is God the Father, God the Son and God the Holy Spirit.

God has many names that reveal His character to us. While researching this I came across a document on the internet saying that there are over 950 names and titles of God. Isn't that incredible? Our God is high above all our understanding and yet He loves us. He loves you and He loves me.

God came to earth as a man, Jesus, so we could relate to Him in a real way. He died an horrific death and rose again from the grave. Now He is alive and seated at the right hand of the Father in heaven, yet He did not leave us alone, He sent the Comforter, Holy Spirit to be here with us and to guide us and lead us through this earthly life. He could have said "no" to the cross, but He made the choice to give His life for you and me so that we could live for all eternity with Him. What sacrificial love is this? It is love like no other. There is no human being that will ever love us this way. This is Jesus, your first love.

God the Father

Our God is love, all encompassing, all that is good and pure and Holy. He is full of majesty, power and glory. There are several descriptions of God in the Bible. He is described as light or a consuming fire. 1 John 1:5 says,

> *"This is the message we have heard from him and declare to you: God is light; in him there is no darkness at all."*

I love Habakkuk's portrayal of God in Habakkuk 3:3-6:

> *"His glory covered the heavens, and His praise filled the earth. His splendour was like the sunrise, rays flashed from His hand, where His power was hidden, plague went before Him, pestilence followed His steps. He stood and shook the earth; He looked and made the nations tremble. The ancient mountains crumbled, and the age-old hills collapsed, but He marches on forever".*

Wow! How amazing is our God, we cannot begin to imagine. He is unfathomable, awesome in power. There are no words. He is the great **I AM**, existing for all time and yet outside of time. The beginning and the end; Alpha and Omega.

Jesus the Son

He was with God at the beginning. The image of our invisible God. Our Saviour, our Lord, our mediator, our friend, our redeemer, the Light of the world. The anointed one, the good shepherd, bread of life, healer and Holy One. The Way, the Truth and the Life. The sinless Lamb of God, the Prince of Peace, gentle as a lamb and ferocious as a lion. What more can I say? In both Daniel and Revelation there are incredible descriptions of Him. Daniel 7:9 reads,

> *"As I looked, thrones were set in place, and the Ancient of Days took His seat. His clothing was as white as snow; the hair of His head was white like wool. His throne was flaming with fire, and its wheels were all ablaze."*

Revelation 1:14 says,

> *"The hair on His head was white like wool, as white as snow, and His eyes were like blazing fire".*

Thank you, Jesus, for laying down Your life for me. I love you Jesus. What way can I thank You, but by laying down my own life for You.

Holy Spirit

Holy Spirit, like Jesus, was with God in the beginning. The third part of the Trinity. He is my guide, my strength and my comforter. He bears fruit in my life if I allow him to work in me and through me. He equips me with all spiritual gifts. He is the power of the Living God and also, He is my friend. As I work together in partnership with Him, He enables me to live a Holy life, set apart for Him and for His purposes. Without Him I am nothing. He is my inner conscience and corrector when I wander off track. He reveals my hidden sin and helps me to live the righteous life I am called to. When I walk closely with Him, I can do all God asks of me. I can surrender, I can overcome, I can forgive, and I can love those the world sees as unlovable. He enables me to live the full life that God intended for me. Acts 1:8 says,

> *"But you will receive power when the Holy Spirit comes on you; and you will be My witnesses in Jerusalem and in Judea and Samaria, and to the ends of the earth".*

John 14:26 reads,

> *"But the advocate, the Holy Spirit, whom the Father will send in My name will teach you all things and will remind you of everything I have said to you".*

There is so much more to say... if you will pick up your Bible and read awhile then you will see I have merely scratched the surface.

Faith is an action word!

As I have been writing, God has been speaking to me about Faith - about what it really is. He keeps telling me the same thing over and over in different ways. The Collins Dictionary definition is this -

- A strong or unshakeable belief in something, especially without proof or evidence.
- A conviction of the truth of certain doctrines of religion, especially when this is not based on reason.
- Complete confidence or trust in a person.

A Biblical definition of faith is often taken from Hebrews 11:1:

> *"Now faith is the confidence in what we hope for and the assurance about what we do not see."*

God has been showing me recently that faith is much more than this. We can believe in something and yet still not have faith in it. We can be told about Jesus and believe what we are told but unless we act on what we believe then it is not faith. As an example, think of a chair. We can have a chair in front of us to sit on. We know it is a chair, and we can believe it is strong enough to take our weight, but until we actually sit on it, we are not operating in faith. Faith in the chair comes in the action of sitting on the chair, faith that it will hold us.

The Greek word used most often in the New Testament for faith is - "pistis". It indicates a belief, a conviction with the addition of trust. Faith is not merely an intellectual concept, but a belief that leads us to action. James 2:26 reads,

> *"As the body without the spirit is dead, so faith without deeds is dead".*

James talks about demonstrating our faith by our works, what we actually do speaks louder than what we say. Faith is an active trust in God. As we believe what He says is true, this should result in action from us. We believe that we are sinners saved by Grace. Because we believe this, we are able to put our trust in Him and hand over the control of our lives. For, if we have died with Christ, then it is no longer we that live, but Christ displaying His life in us through faith.

Some years ago, I was working for a local church as treasurer and administrator. So of course, I was aware of the financial situation of the church at that time. I knew the church could no longer afford to pay my salary. I felt God speak to me about giving up my salary whilst continuing to do the work. In the natural Ali and I felt it would put a strain on our own financial situation, but we prayed about it and trusted God to supply all our personal needs. It was a step of faith. We trusted God to move in the situation and He did. If we believe God's word to be true, that He will supply ALL our needs through Christ Jesus, then we can take a step of faith because we understand who He is, and that He will not let us down. In taking this step of faith we needed courage and the strength to trust God and take Him at His word. Guess what, everything was OK, our God is faithful.

Faith, then, is not just a feeling or a belief. Faith is acting upon what we believe to be true. As Holy Spirit challenges and nudges us, we must ask ourselves if we really believe what God tells us in His Word. If we do, then there will be times when we will need all our God-given strength and courage to step out in faith to do the things He is calling us to do. Just like we did when we first heard the gospel message and gave our lives to Jesus, we have to do something.

Each day we need to exercise our faith, in the same way as we exercise our muscles. The more we do this, the more our faith grows. We need to act on what we believe to be true. If God speaks to us, we need to respond. If He reveals an issue in our life that needs to be addressed, we need to trust Him and then do something about it. We cannot ignore God. If we do not act on what He is showing us through Holy Spirit, we are not exercising our faith. Eventually our faith will become weak and dwindle away and we may even lose our faith. When this happens, we begin to live our lives for ourselves again. We revert back to how things used to be. We compromise, and our life no longer lines up to God's plumbline. In other words, we start to look less and less like Jesus.

Why am I telling you this? I believe that we are in the end-of-the end-days and so we are going to need faith more than we've ever needed it before. God is looking for His church to have faith and to stand in this final generation. The world is growing darker by the day and now is the time for the church to become real. We need to shine bright as this world gets darker. No more sitting on the fence, no more having one foot in the world and one in the Kingdom. God wants all of you and all of me! We may be called upon to lay down our lives in the same way that Jesus laid down His life for us. Are you prepared for that? If not, are you willing to be made willing?

An Invitation from God

I believe the Lord is sending out heavenly invitations to all His children, asking them to get involved in the great move of God that is coming. Will you say 'yes'? Will you enter into all He has for you to do in these last days? How will your invitation arrive? It may surprise you. It could even be this book! God is asking more of His people, He wants us all to answer the call. If you are to answer 'yes' to the invitation you will need to have courage and to trust Him like never before.

I have received my invitation and I have said 'yes'. There is no turning back for me now. I will have to make sacrifices and no doubt endure suffering in the future, as will you. Yet I know I can trust my Lord and that I cannot say no. I am right at the beginning of a new and exciting stage of my Christian journey. I trust Jesus more now than ever before. He is growing in me in ways I have never experienced before. My first assignment is - this book!

Jesus tells us that in the last days many will turn away from Him and betray and hate each other. He tells us many will be deceived. Matthew 24: 9-14 [NLT] reads,

> *"Then you will be arrested, persecuted and killed. You will be hated all over the world because you are my followers. And many will turn away from Me and betray and hate each other. And many false prophets will appear and deceive many people. Sin will be rampant everywhere, and the love of many will grow cold. But the one who endures to the end will be saved. And the Good News about the Kingdom will be preached throughout the whole world, so that all nations will hear it, and then the end will come".*

It is God's desire that none should fall away. Yet, the love of many will grow cold. He wants you to remain strong, to be more courageous than you've ever been. This is not the time to stand back or to shy away. It is time to accept your invitation when it arrives. He is calling you.

There will be times when you may sense God is challenging you, and you may be uncomfortable or overwhelmed. Pause in those moments and trust God, the author and finisher of your faith. Remember your first love. That special touch from the Holy Spirit that gave you so much joy. It will be enough to spur you on to greater deeds, to say yes to His invitation.

My Invitation

My invitation came on the 25th of July 2021 as I sat quietly waiting on Him.

> *"A time is coming when the hearts of My people will be laid bare. I will consume them with My Holy fire, burning up all that is not*

of Me. For those who are willing I will cleanse and purge their hearts. It will be painful, but in those moments, I will remove all contamination that has accumulated since conception. These ones will be remade Holy and pure, and I will consume them with my Light and cover them with my Glory. There will be no going back for them. These will be My light carriers. I am preparing them now, drawing them in to the place of total surrender. I am looking for those who are prepared to step out of the world, who are willing to separate themselves from any further contamination. They will be wise and have increased discernment. They will have eyes to see and ears to hear what I am saying in these days. These are the burning ones, and My Holy fire will be carried by them and will burn up all that they collect that is contaminated as they walk through these days by My side. No longer will they pilot their own lives. I, the Lord, will be their pilot. I will plot their course and plan their times. The flesh life will be consumed by the burning fire they carry. This call is heavy and there is a cost. Do you want it? Say 'yes'!"

As I wrote these words, I was not initially aware of the heaviness of them, but, as I read through them again, I understood the enormity of the calling. I knew I had to say 'yes'. I could not walk away from the call. I could not say no to my God. I am all in. There is no turning back for me.

So, when I falter, or when I feel like giving up, when times are tough, I will always return to my first love and remind myself what this is all about. What Jesus did for me made my life worth something. I have hope, I have vision, I have purpose. Now I also have the freedom to become the person I was created to be. I will set my heart upon Him, to do His will, from now until He takes me home. He is my first love. My life with Him is eternal.

So.....are you prepared for YOUR invitation?

GET READY

It's all about the Heart

What exactly is the heart?

This is not an easy question to answer, and I am not a Bible scholar, though I will very briefly have a look at this from my limited understanding. One thing I do know is that if we read the scriptures, we cannot get away from the heart, it is mentioned at least 1,000 times in the Bible; that's a lot! If it is mentioned so often it must be very important. One of my favourite scriptures about the heart is found in Proverbs 4:23:

> *"Above all else, guard your heart, for everything you do flows from it".*

So, when the Bible talks about the heart, what is it referring to? In the modern day, 21st century, when we hear the word 'heart' we will probably think of the physical heart, the vital organ in our body that pumps the blood around our bodies. In the ancient world when the Bible was written, a few thousand years ago, they did not have the same understanding of anatomy and physiology that we have today. We have the advantage of years of research and study of scholars and scientists. We have learnt in school, in biology classes, about the heart and how important it is to the functioning of our physical body. Those who wrote the ancient writings had quite a different understanding to us. It was believed that the origin of thoughts came from somewhere around the area of our stomach, somewhere near the centre of our bodies. They did not have the same understanding about thought processes that we do today. In the scriptures when they talk about the heart, they really mean the mind.

The Hebrew word that is often translated as 'heart' is the word 'leb' and it would probably be better translated as mind.

Strong's concordance says this,

> **Definition 'Leb':** *"inner man", "mind", "will", "heart"*
> **'Lebab':** *"heart" (the most interior organ), "being", "think in themselves", "breast", "comfortably", "courage", "midst", "mind", "unawares", "understanding"*

An absolutely fascinating discovery has been made in recent years as neuroscience has advanced, it is about the human heart and the brain. It appears that there are neurons in the heart that actually connect to the brain.

When we read the word 'heart' in scripture we should probably think more about our will, our mind, our consciousness, our emotions, and our understanding. Our heart could be described as the place of knowing, memory, and reflection. We know that these processes take place in our brain, and we now also know that our brain and heart are connected. Isn't it incredible that when the Bible was written all those years ago, these things were not known or understood? But they still wrote using the word 'heart'

Let us now have a very quick look at the Greek word translated as 'heart'. Strong's concordance says this:

> **Kardia:** "the heart", "mind", "character"," inner self", "will", "intention", "centre".

Our word, 'cardiac' comes from here.

I would just like to look at a couple of examples in scripture where the word heart is used. To show how heart and mind are the same thing.

Jeremiah 29:13 reads,

"You will seek me and find me when you seek me with all your 'heart.'

We know that this makes more sense if we use the word mind. If we are looking for something, we think about it and use our brain, our intellect. We would probably not use the word heart here if we were writing today.

2 Corinthians 9:7 says,

> *"Each of you should give what you have decided in your "heart" to give, not reluctantly or under compulsion, for God loves a cheerful giver".*

Here Paul is telling the Christians in Corinth that they should consider how much they wanted to give. We know that this is something we would think about with our brain, our intellect. We would also pray about it and ask Holy Spirit to guide us in our thinking. In our physical being it would be our brain that we would use, not our heart.

After saying all of that we, as Spirit filled believers, would probably say 'heart' when talking about these things, as we have become accustomed to how the scripture is written, and Holy Spirit has given us a better understanding in our spirits of these things. Our head has connected with our heart. These things are difficult to put on paper as they are spiritual understandings but those reading, who have the Spirit of God residing within, will undoubtedly know what I am saying here.

Our heart is at the centre of our being. It is the deepest part of our soul, it is the crux of who we are. It is often described as the seat of our affections or feelings. It is where our character is developed. The fruit of the spirit is produced in our heart by Holy Spirit. This fruit of the spirit - love, joy, peace, patience, kindness, goodness, faithfulness, gentleness, and self-control are all there. We all have this fruit within us, as we work with Holy Spirit and live our lives exercising and displaying the fruit. It will grow and will become more of a natural outflow from deep within our beings.

The Bible also tells us that we are all born with iniquity within our hearts, Psalm 51:5 says,

> *"Surely I was sinful at birth, sinful from the time my mother conceived me."*

Iniquity, the root of all sin is also there in our hearts, from the day we were conceived. Sin is the fruit of iniquity. The more we sin, the deeper the root of iniquity grows.

It could be said that our heart is the home of our moral life, and it produces our character. It may be described as a good, kind, gentle, loving heart, or a cold, hard or selfish heart. This is dependent on which part of our heart we focus on or which part we exercise the most. The more we exercise in sin the stronger the iniquity becomes. If, however, we work in partnership with Holy Spirit, and deal with iniquity as it arises, exercising the fruit of Holy Spirit in our lives then more fruit will be released and that is what will be evident in our character.

Because of the iniquity in our hearts, it is possible for us to make ungodly decisions about how we live our life. All the thoughts we have and decisions we make are influenced by the environment we live in, the people we associate with, the things we listen to and the things we look at. These influences, good or bad, enter our hearts via our physical senses. All our thought processes and decision making takes place within our souls. This is where decisions are formulated, and we then act upon the decisions we make. The actions we take may be good or bad. We are able to make good decisions and live good lives, if we have good and positive influences in the world, but we will always pick up contamination from the world we live in. It is inevitable.

When we become Christians, the Spirit of God comes to reside within us. We have actually taken on the righteousness of Christ. We now have everything we need to live a righteous life. Once we activate Holy Spirit within us by praying for Him to fill us, the gifts of the Spirit and everything else available to us from Holy Spirit, flows from our spirit into our hearts. We can now make good godly decisions about how we live our lives. All these things now flow from our heart into our soul, and we can now make decisions and act out of the overflow of the good things the spirit of God has placed within us. Because of the iniquity within our hearts and the contamination we receive from external influences in the world there is always going to be a battle. We have to choose and make decisions about the external influences that we allow to affect us and the way we live our lives. We make choices every day, and by the power of the Spirit of God that resides in us we can make godly choices. We also have iniquity that is rooted deep within, and we have to remember there is an enemy of our soul prowling around. It is a guarantee that he will send temptation our way. We must be strong enough in our faith to stand against any temptation the enemy throws at us. It is so important that we fully know and understand who we are in Jesus Christ and who He is in us?

Circumcision of the Heart

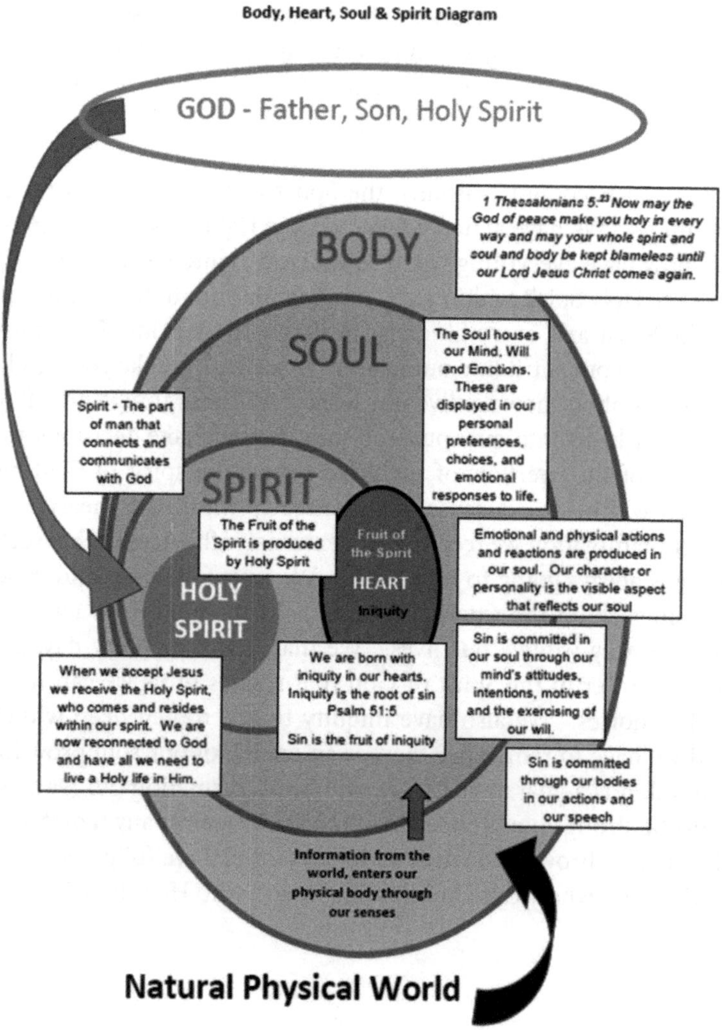

Pearl Blake July 2008

My Christian journey has been very much focused on the 'heart'. Around the year 2000, God gave me a series of three pictures relating to the heart. These pictures came over a period of a few months and have been central to my Christian journey ever since. I will try to put into words what the Lord showed me during that time.

In the first picture I saw a dry riverbed. The riverbed was in the bottom of a valley with steep cliffs forming each side of the valley. At the head of the valley was God's thumb which was holding back the waters from the river above, stopping the water from flowing down into the valley below. On the valley floor, in the dry riverbed was a human heart. God's other hand was holding a scalpel above the heart.

I was reminded in that moment of the scripture in Deuteronomy 30:6:

> *"The LORD your God will circumcise your hearts and the hearts of your descendants, so that you may love him with all your heart and with all your soul, and live."*

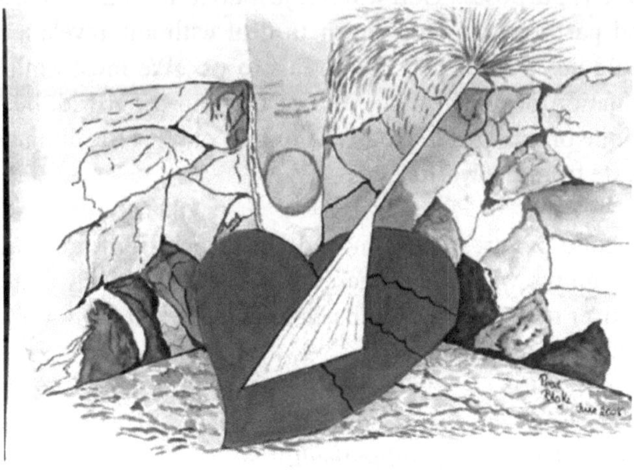

Pearl Blake July 2008

What does it mean to circumcise our heart? Circumcision literally means to cut. This was done when making a covenant with God. The Abrahamic covenant was sealed by circumcision. This physical circumcision preceded circumcision of the heart.

Circumcision of the heart is twofold. Firstly, we are figuratively laying down our lives on the operating table of God and allowing God to cut open our hearts with His holy scalpel, to cut away and remove all the contamination within. We are making a covenant with God saying that our hearts are His and we are open for Him to do whatever is needed to keep them pure. If you remember, covenants are two-way agreements. As we agree for God to work in our hearts, we also have our part to play, and we have to work with Him and walk in obedience. We have to do the things He asks of us in order to maintain purity of heart.

I believe the picture I received from God was a call to purity, to me personally, and also to the Church. God's desire is that we surrender totally to Him, that we die to ourselves, that we lay down our lives and allow Him to do whatever is necessary to make us pure and Holy. It is a call to sanctification, a call for us to be Holy and set apart for His purposes. God will not just do it, we must work with Him and partner with Holy Spirit to deal with any revelation of sin or iniquity within, that He reveals to us. We must limit the contamination of our hearts. We must live in the world, but we must not be of the world. God is calling us out. He is calling us to be separate from the world.

In the second picture, God removed His thumb from the head of the river and the water was released. I knew instinctively that this was the River of Life, which is talked about in Ezekiel 47, Revelation 22 and John 7:38 which says,

> *"Whoever believes in me, as Scripture has said, rivers of living water will flow from within them."*

I saw the water start to fall over the cliff edge, it poured into the back of the new, pure, white heart. It flowed through the heart and gushed out of the front. It was powerful, pure clean water, gushing forth from this pure white heart, bringing life and power and healing with it.

God was showing me that there is a promise to those who walk in obedience and respond to this call of separation, to those who accept the invitation to stand with Him in this final generation. He promises to remove His thumb from the head of the valley and to release the Rivers of Life in and through the pure hearts that have been laid bare before Him.

In the third picture, the heart was being carried away on the crest of a wave, it was going where the river flowed and was pouring out the pure living water as it went.

God said to me that He was going to carry those ones with Him into many places far and wide. There was no battle or struggle, it was easy for them to be carried along on the crest of the wave. It was as if they were flying, no resistance, no sinking, just flowing. He will take them away with Him. The living water will continue to flow from them and affect the world around them wherever He takes them.

Like I said earlier, these pictures have never left me and I have lived my life always trying to honour God. Many times I have laid down on the operating table and asked God to do what is necessary to purify my heart. He always does. I don't believe I have yet seen the full release of His thumb with the resulting torrent of living water flowing in and through me. I believe it is coming, I believe God is calling us to a new level of intimacy with Him in this new era in these end-of-the-end-days. It is intense, there is no turning back. He wants to take us deeper and higher with Him.

Seeing into Hearts

A time is coming when those believers who have been working in partnership with Holy Spirit and are being sanctified will be able to look into people's eyes and see deep into their hearts. They will see the hurt and the pain that has been buried for far too long. This will enable the saints to speak truth and life, healing and wholeness, cleansing, and purity into these souls. In Luke 11:34, we read,

> *"Your eye is the lamp of your body. When your eyes are healthy, your whole body also is full of light. But when they are unhealthy, your body also is full of darkness."*

Where are you?

Are you one of these saints who is in the process of being purified? Is Holy Spirit working in you and healing and purifying every part of your being, preparing you as part of His bride and making you ready for His return? As you move forward and continue in this process you will begin to know things are changing. You will feel different, you will be different, others will see changes in you. You will start to see into people's hearts in a way you haven't done before. Move in the new things that are being released in you, step out in faith knowing that God has plans for you in this new era to unlock hearts and release captives. Trust the Lord that He is doing a new thing, don't be afraid. Be strong and have courage to do the things Holy Spirit is asking you to do.

Maybe you know that you have not started on this journey yet. If this is you, I pray that you will be able to open up your heart in a deeper way than ever before and that you will allow Holy Spirit to move? I pray you will be brave, and you will lay your heart bare on the operating table of the Lord. It is time to be honest with yourself and get real before Him. Remember He can see deep into your being and knows everything about you, nothing is hidden from Him. Now is the time to open up completely. There is not much time left, there is so much work to be done. It is the time of purification. Do you choose to be purified, to be sanctified, set apart and holy for His purposes? Or are you happy to stay as you are?

Cry out today from the depths of your very being and tell Father God just how you feel, be honest, be real. Although He is all-knowing and knows what you think and feel, He wants to hear you cry out to Him, He wants you to want more of Him. He wants to hear you say 'yes' to Him. This is an invitation from God to you. What will your response be?

Deeper and Higher

I believe we are living in a day when God is calling His children to a deeper place, a deeper place of intimacy with Him. It tells us in Psalm 42:7:

> *"Deep calls to deep in the roar of your waterfalls, all your waves and breakers have swept over me."*

A place at the depths of our being calls out to the depths of our God and to places that are outside of our human thinking or understanding. We may be at the depths of ourselves, in as much as we are desperate and have a deep desire to know Him more. To be able to commune with Him on a different level, at a greater depth and intensity than we have ever done before. Or, it may be that we are at the end of ourselves, in a place of brokenness and deep despair, just as David was, and we are needing Him to intervene. We're crying out to Him from our very being in pain and desperation. Either way, we have a deep desire for God's presence, we know there is so much more. We are living in a day when God is calling us to a much deeper place in Him.

James Smith and Robert Lee in Handfuls on Purpose for Christian Workers and Bible Students: "deep calls to deep" say this,

> *"The deep of man's need calls unto the deep of God's fulness; and the deep of God's fulness calls unto the deep of man's need.*

> *Between our emptiness and His all-sufficiency there is a great gulf. . . Deep calls unto deep. The deep mercy of God needs our emptiness, into which it might pour itself. . . Nothing can fully meet the depth of our need but the depth of His Almighty fulness."*
>
> (Grand Rapids, Michigan: William B. Eerdmans Publishing Company, 1971. Vol. 8, p.11.)

It is time for that great void within us to be completely filled by the great depths of The Almighty God.

Ezekiel 47 is an incredible passage of scripture, a foundational scripture in my Christian journey. It talks of the river of life that flows from beneath the throne room. As the river flows it gets deeper and deeper. This is a scripture that calls us to jump into the river, to be totally out of our depth in the full flow of the river of life. As I read, I want to dive in, headfirst and feel the power of the river, the refreshing that the water brings, the feeling of exhilaration as I am swept along in this river that brings life. Psalm 42:1-2 says,

> *"As the deer pants for streams of water, so my soul pants for you, my God."*

Are you desperate, like the deer that pants for the streams of water, so thirsty that you might die if you do not get the water you need?

God is calling us deeper, much deeper. He is calling from the very depths of Himself to the very depths of our beings. Are you ready?

He is also calling us to a higher place, a place of deep intimacy with Him; a place where secrets are shared. In this place we find His presence, and in His presence, He reveals to us the secrets of His heart. In His presence is power, in His presence is healing, in His presence is wholeness and oneness. Here we find who we are in Him, we truly find ourselves in His presence. Revelation 4:1 reads,

> *"After this I looked, and there before me was a door standing*

> *open in heaven. And the voice I had first heard speaking to me like a trumpet said, "Come up here, and I will show you what must take place after this."*

When we go deeper, He takes us higher. They seem like opposites, but they are intrinsically connected. As we submit our lives totally to Jesus, we get lower and lay down all those things that we hold so close. As we get desperate for more of Him and seek Him in the deepest place of our hearts, we can jump in headfirst and learn to be out of our depth. We need to learn to breathe under the water and allow it to envelope us, as we let go of our own lives and our own desires. This is when Jesus will take us into the higher place of His Holy presence. As we are sanctified, holy and set apart for His purposes, we are enabled to live righteous lives honouring God in EVERYTHING and we are positioned to go higher. He wants us to join Him in the throne room in the heavenly places, as in Revelation 4. When John went up, the door was open, and it is still open. He wants to take those who seek Him in the deepest place and who allow Him to take total control, those who go deep down in the river and are totally consumed by Him; those who allow the waterfall to wash over them, who get totally out of their depth and allow the Spirit of God to cleanse and purge them; those who trust Him completely and utterly with everything they have and all that they are. He will gather those ones up into that higher place. It is in this place that He will reveal the secrets of His heart.

I believe that God wants to reveal His secrets to His children. Jeremiah 33:3 says,

> *"Call to me and I will answer you, and I will tell you the great and unsearchable things you do not know."*

Daniel 2:22 reads,

> *"He reveals deep and hidden things; he knows what lies in darkness, and light dwells with him. "*

But it will not be an easy place to be. We will hear things that are hard to hear, and we will need to respond to the things that He is revealing to us, the secrets that He is making known. We will need to be ready and know how to respond to the things that He is going to tell us. Just like the men of Issachar in 1 Chronicles 12:32:

> *"From Issachar, men who understood the signs of the times and knew what Israel ought to do".*

In these days we need much greater wisdom, understanding, clarity, knowledge and discernment to be able to know what to do. Where does that come from? It comes from the Lord, from spending time in that deep place with Him. It comes from listening to Him, learning and yearning to understand more. Until we know what to do with the things that He wants to reveal to us, God will not take us to that higher place where His secrets will be revealed.

So again, there is a need to go deeper, from the depths of our own understanding in order for us to glean, learn from and experience the depths of God. We need to be open and willing to learn new things in Him. We need to open our minds in these end-of-the-end days. We may be surprised at some of the things He wants to teach us. Let us not be afraid. If our hearts are truly His, He will only lead us down good and righteous paths. He will not allow us to be deceived. We just have to say yes.

A Divine Exchange

We have heard of the divine exchange, where Jesus died on the cross and gave up His life so we could live. This is like a further divine exchange where we get to the bottom of ourselves or the end of ourselves, and God passes knowledge, wisdom, understanding and the secrets of His heart over to us in a divine exchange, our emptiness for the fullness of Himself.

Psalm 42:7 says,

> *"Deep calls to deep"*

It is time for the church to arise, to wake up and to listen to the things He has to say in these days. We need to be free from all that binds us and holds us back from being totally free in Him. He wants to reveal His plans to us, the secrets of His heart, but we need to go higher in order to receive these things. Our tethers need cutting; we need releasing to be able to fly high. Amos 3:7 says,

> *"Surely the sovereign Lord does nothing without revealing His plan to His servants the prophets."*

Sifting of the Church

The church is being sifted, many are starting to fall away, many will not want to pay the price or to make the necessary sacrifices and so they will walk away for an easier life. Matthew 24:10-13 reads,

> *"At that time many will turn away from the faith and will betray and hate each other, and many false prophets will appear and deceive many people. Because of the increase of wickedness, the love of most will grow cold, but the one who stands firm to the end will be saved."*

We are hearing of several "Big Christian names" saying they are no longer Christians. I have heard it said that people are deconstructing their faith. This is another sign of the times we are living in. Many will fall away. If we are hearing about people who have been prominent leaders in the Church falling away, then how many more are there that we don't hear about?

Treasure in heaven

Nothing on this earth is for ever, it is all temporary and we are on earth for a short time. We will be alive with our Lord and Saviour for eternity. Matthew 24:35 tells us that "Heaven and earth will pass away" and 2 Peter 3:13 tells us, "We are waiting for new heavens and a new earth in which righteousness dwells." When you look at these scriptures and then look at the whole global warming and climate change issue it is important that we get it all into perspective. Yes, be good stewards but do not make the planet your God.

So why hold on to our earthly life? We know that our time on earth is temporary and we may enjoy things and entertain things that are not godly because they please us in the moment , but we must think of our eternal existence. However many years we may have left, is it worth sacrificing our eternity?

It's time to let go of all of our earthly desires and to give God everything. He wants our all, nothing less will do. Luke 9:24 reads,

> *"For whoever wants to save their life will lose it, but whoever loses their life for me will save it."*

Those who are ready and willing to make the necessary sacrifices here and now, for them there is a great reward awaiting on that glorious day. Let us not forget that our treasures are in heaven. In Matthew 6:20 it says,

> *"Store up for yourselves treasures in heaven...."*

In Matthew 19:16-30 we have a young man who is rich and has his whole life ahead of him. He is a ruler, a man of nobility, but he knows he is lacking. He comes to Jesus and asks, "Good teacher, what good thing shall I do that I may have eternal life?" Jesus says to him, "If you want to enter into eternal life, keep the commandments." The young man responds by asking Jesus which commandments he should keep, and Jesus responds by listing some of them. The young man is quick to reply and tells Jesus that he has kept all these commandments from being young, but asks what do I still lack?

He knew he was still lacking in some area, even though he kept the commandments. Jesus' response was not what the young man wanted to hear. Jesus replied, "If you want to be perfect, go, sell what you have and give to the poor, and you will have treasure in heaven; and come follow me." What did the young man do? He walked away from Jesus. This is so sad. That young man could not bear to walk away from his earthly wealth and lifestyle, he was not prepared to sacrifice anything; he was happy to keep the commandments as that didn't really cost him anything, but not prepared to do what was needed to enter the Kingdom of heaven and have eternal life. This young man was ready to enter the dust when he died his physical death and rot, rather than live a life of eternity with His Father in heaven. How very sad! He knew there was an eternity, as that was his initial question to Jesus, but he was not prepared for the cost.

How many of us are like that, how many of us are not really prepared to pay the price? We would rather risk our eternity with Father God than live a life of total obedience and surrender to Him. Just because our fleeting earthly desires seem, in the moment, to be more attractive. No one said when we accepted Jesus, that it would be easy. If they did, they lied! That is a false gospel. Following Jesus wholeheartedly has a cost, there is a price to pay, it is a lifelong commitment. We have all we need to live a life honouring God in all things by the power of Holy Spirit. Don't be tempted by earthly desires that seem attractive in the moment, money, sex, drink and drugs, and anything else that takes us away from Jesus.

Jesus' disciples had been listening intently. When Jesus told this story He turned to them and said, *"I tell you the truth, it is hard for a rich man to enter the kingdom of heaven. It is easier for a camel to pass through the eye of a needle than for a rich man to enter the kingdom of God." The disciples were shocked by this and asked, "Who then can be saved?" Jesus said, "With men this is impossible, but with God all things are possible."*

Peter answered, "We have left all and followed you! What then will there be for us?" Jesus said, "I tell you the truth, at the renewal of all things, when the Son of Man sits on His glorious throne, you who have followed me will also sit on twelve thrones, judging the twelve tribes of Israel. And everyone who has left houses or brothers or sisters of father or mother or children or fields for my sake will receive a hundred times as much and will inherit eternal life. But many who are first will be last, and many who are last will be first." (Mathew 19:23-30.)

There is an encouragement here for you and for me. The sacrifices we make in order to follow Jesus wholeheartedly, will be rewarded. All that we give up, all that it costs in time, finances, or any other way, to enable us to do the things He has called us to do, will be rewarded one day in eternity, when we will rule with King Jesus.

There is another encouragement for us in Matthew 6:19-21. Jesus says,

> *"Do not store up for yourselves treasures on earth, where moths and vermin destroy, and where thieves break in and steal. But store up for yourselves treasures in heaven, where moths and vermin do not destroy, and where thieves do not break in and steal. For where your treasure is, there your heart will be also."*

Our treasures are being built up for us in heaven and one day we will be spiritually very rich. I believe that our heavenly riches will be far more valuable than any earthly riches we may ever have.

I understand what it is like to make sacrifices in order to be obedient to the Lord. We all make sacrifices on a daily basis to serve Him in order to see God's kingdom built. Imagine how God feels about your sacrifice, He weeps when He sees your heart to serve Him. He is thrilled when He sees you laying down your earthly lives to follow Him.

Be encouraged, continue doing the things the Lord has called you to do, without question, without hesitation, without any expectation of any earthly recompense but with the knowledge that your treasure is building up in heaven.

It is no longer enough for us to sing nice songs on a Sunday and to go home and continue living the lives that compromise our faith. We can no longer hide away in a big congregation and just enjoy the social atmosphere of church, talking the talk but not walking the walk.

God is raising up the true Church, the real believers, those who are serious about Him. The Remnant Church. He is raising up His Church in this new era, in these end-of-the-end days. Those who continue to hold on to things that are not righteous in their lives may fall away or could be deceived and used by the enemy. Let us remember that we were made righteous when we were saved. God gave us all His righteousness. Righteousness is the outworking of holiness. One who is holy lives a righteous life. Although we were given the righteousness of Christ, we often do not live righteous lives. If we are not holy, we cannot live righteously. We need to live right with God. Again, some people see this as a salvation of works, but that is not true. The only way of salvation is through Jesus, accepting Him as Lord. You cannot be saved by doing good works. However, once a person is truly saved, they receive the righteousness of Christ and, so now, they are equipped to live righteous lives in Him. They should aim to live lives that are right in His eyes. True salvation will have some evidence of a life transformation. If that is not evident then salvation could be questioned.

If we, the Church, the Body of Christ, are not ready to be made spotless; if we are not prepared to get rid of our blemishes; if we are not willing to be made holy as He is holy; and, if we are not prepared to live righteous lives as we are called to do, we will not survive. Ephesians 5:27 says,

"... and to present her to himself as a radiant church, without stain or wrinkle or any other blemish, but holy and blameless."

1 Peter 1:16 says,

"For it is written, be holy because I am holy"

If we are not willing and prepared to make all the changes necessary in our own personal lives, if we are not willing to give up things that hinder our relationship with Jesus, these things can close down our intimacy with Him. Unless we put ourselves in to situations where we will be challenged or made to feel uncomfortable, the Spirit of God cannot shine His light into our hearts or reveal the darkness within.

Unless we are prepared for our hearts to be laid bare, for our hearts to be circumcised, cut open and cleaned out, then we are never going to be able to receive the things from God we will need in order to survive in the difficult days that lie ahead for us as His Church. Let's always remember that God's word says in 1 Corinthians 10:13:

"No temptation has overtaken you except what is common to mankind. And God is faithful; he will not let you be tempted beyond what you can bear. But when you are tempted, he will also provide a way out so that you can endure it."

He will not give us more than we can cope with, He will give us a way through, but we need to endure, we need to be strong. This Christian journey is based on a relationship with Jesus Christ and so it is a two-way thing. A relationship that is one-sided will always fail. God provides all we need but we must work with Holy Spirit to be in a place to receive. We have to position ourselves to take what He is offering. He will not give if we are not ready. He will not pour into a dirty vessel. If He does, what is then poured out is contaminated and dirty and would cause more harm than good. God is a good God, and His will is not to cause harm. We are contaminated and can cause harm in His name without even knowing we are doing so, believing all the time we are doing good. We must be pure and clean vessels, holy and set apart for His purposes. Let us get ready for what He is about to do. Deep is crying to deep, let us partake in this divine exchange and go higher with Him. There is so much more for us; we have seen nothing yet. Let us go higher and then we can receive the secrets of His heart.

Seeing the Hearts of People

In these days the Lord will show us the hearts of people. We will look into their eyes and see their hearts. He will show us the hearts of both the saved and the unsaved, but it is not for us to judge, but for us to minister more effectively in the power of Holy Spirit.

I believe that there are men and women today masquerading as Christians. They are fake, they are counterfeit Christians. Some may be deliberately doing this because they see some benefit for themselves, fame or money, or power even. There are others that really believe themselves to be Christian but, unfortunately, they have been deceived by a wrong theology, or they are not prepared to deal with their own hearts. Whichever category they fall into they are not operating in the truth, love and power of God. Because of this people get hurt and the Body of Christ suffers as a result.

These vessels are not clean, and we need to understand that God will not pour anything into a dirty, unclean vessel. What happens in these instances is the enemy jumps in as the great deceiver making them look like the real deal, but they are counterfeit. Many of these believe they are operating in the truth, but they are deceived and they, in turn, deceive others.

Be aware of counterfeit

Dont allow the enemy to deceive you by either using you as a counterfeit Christian or by using counterfeit Christians to deceive you to buy into something that is not of God. Be sure to guard your heart. If you believe you are working for the Living God, but know you have unresolved sin in your heart, do not be deceived. Matthew 24:11 says,

> *".... and many false prophets will appear and deceive many."*

Acts 20:30:

> *"Even from your own number men will arise and distort the truth in order to draw away disciples after them".*

If you are a Christian ministering in Jesus' name, please, I urge you, to continually check your heart and deal immediately with any iniquity that the Spirit of God may reveal to you. We have to work with Him, believe and have faith and trust Him. He knows what He is doing. If we aim to be obedient in all things at all times, He will give us all we need to live a full life and to endure to the end. If we present a pure and clean vessel before Him, He will fill it with good and wholesome gifts that will enable us to endure to the end, and to bring light into the dark world around us as we journey with Him.

If we are not prepared to deal with iniquity, then it is best not to minister in the name of Jesus. Be honest with yourself and with God. Step back, step down and allow the Holy Spirit of God to minister to you in the areas that need cleansing. Allow Him to bring restoration and then, when He says it is time, you can step back into ministry.

If we continue to live with patches of darkness within, in the form of jealousy, unforgiveness, rebellion, sexual immorality, pride, self-righteousness, selfishness, love of money, materialism and laziness or anything else that pleases and gratifies us but does not please or honour God, He will not honour us. If we are not willing to deal with these things that the Spirit of God reveals, then we will never be ready! If we are ministering to others in the name of Jesus whilst in this condition we may be harming them rather than helping them. How can we help others to be ready if we are not ready ourselves.

In order for us to receive the things of God, needed to enable us to survive in these last days, we need to be clean and pure vessels, ready for Him to pour into us so we can be poured out. We will not survive the things that are ahead; we will not be able to stand against the persecution that is coming our way; we will not endure; and we will NOT be ready for Jesus.

Those ministering in Jesus' name and refusing to deal with iniquity are living in a dangerous place. Harm can be caused to those we want to help, and we can place our own eternity in jeopardy. Our God is an awesome God, why would we not want to live to please Him?

Jesus is returning for His Bride very soon, sooner than many of us would dare to believe. Life is going to be very difficult for the Church in these coming days. Paul gives us many warnings and many hints to help us to understand these things. We need to finish the race that we are in; we need to work out our salvation with fear and trembling; for we are not fully saved until Jesus returns for His Bride.

We are in a process of being saved. As Christians we have everything necessary to be saved. When we accepted Jesus, we were effectively saved. In that moment we received everything we need to live a life that is pleasing to God. We received Holy Spirit. In Him is all power to live holy lives. We are being saved every day as we live and walk a life of repentance. As we live our lives in partnership with Holy Spirit, according to His leading, we are being saved. We will be fully saved on the day of Jesus coming, when we meet Him in the clouds on that glorious day.

Our journey as Christians, is a journey of salvation and we are working out our salvation each and every day. We are being saved day by day and when Jesus returns for His bride, we will finally be saved. As has been said, "We have been saved; we are being saved; we will be saved.

I feel that the Church has often been OK with complacency. It has seemed acceptable for Church to be more like a social club where people come together to meet friends in a comfortable environment. This is no longer the case.

We are in a new era and our days are numbered. The world is a mess and morality is declining at a speed that is unprecedented. This new era requires that the Church be ready. In the short time that is left God is going to use those ones that are willing to be totally laid down and surrendered and full of light in new and powerful ways.

We will start to understand more about the authority we have in the name of Jesus; we will have confidence and boldness to step out in ways we have never done before; and we will start to see miraculous happenings like never before. God will show us secrets about people, we will see into their hearts, and we will need to act upon the things He shows us.

We need to be determined and resolute in our own life and walk with Jesus. We must not defile our bodies in any way. We need to keep our temples holy and pure so the living water of the Holy Spirit can flow in and through our hearts and will not be contaminated in any way.

We need wisdom and balanced judgment. This will come as we open ourselves up more and more for the Spirit of God to use us, we need wisdom and discretion as we walk in the new gifts that the Lord is releasing upon us.

God will show mercy to those He places before us as He reveals the secrets of their hearts to us. He will do this in order for us to be able to help them as we act upon the secrets that He is showing us. God wants to reveal secrets of other people's hearts to us so that we can get involved and work in partnership with Holy Spirit to see transformation take place in their lives. We will be able to understand people and speak into their lives in a way we have not been able to do before, because we will be able to see into their hearts. We will feel their pain and minister to them with the love of God to bring about healing, deliverance and restoration through the power of Holy Spirit.

God's kingdom is coming and will stand forever. We can be a part of bringing that kingdom into being by living in obedience to the things of God, by opening ourselves up to the Spirit of God, by dealing with the sin in our own hearts and allowing the light of the Lord to consume us, fill us, heal us and release us from the clutches of the enemy. Only then are we ready to move out in this new era to do the things that God is calling us to do.

As we start to move in these new areas of revelation, power and the mysteries of God, others will see and be jealous, and will want to operate in the things of God just as we are. This is a good jealousy as it will drive others to seek out the face of Jesus in ways they have never done before. God said to me, "Lorraine, jealousy stirs my people." In Romans 11:4, Paul said the same thing as he went to preach to the Gentiles. He said that jealousy will drive the Jews to want to know Jesus, their Messiah.

Are you happy for others to see into your heart? Are you willing to be used of God to see into hearts and minister into lives in ways you have never done before?

Physical Healing in the Body of Christ

On 28th July 2021, I had a word from the Lord about Healing:

> "I am bringing a total healing and restoring of souls and physical bodies to those who will answer yes to my invitation, who will lay everything down and be prepared to stand with me in this final generation. We are in the end-of-the-end days, and I am returning for a spotless Bride. You need to be strong in every sense of the word. As well as being strong spiritually, you need to be strong physically. Your physical bodies need to be in good shape and physically fit to do the work I am calling you to. I am going to reset, realign and restore your physical bodies back to factory settings. Just as they were before they became contaminated by the world and by your laziness and lethargy. You need to work with Holy Spirit. As He heals, you must maintain your newly restored bodies. You need to eat well, maintain a healthy weight, and exercise and keep a good level of physical fitness. Holy Spirit will heal, and with His help, you will maintain what He has done."

We are living in exciting times. God is restoring His people, He is healing His Body. We have a mission ahead of us. He is getting us ready, spiritually, emotionally and physically. We must be ready in every area, ready for the assignment He has for us. When we lay our lives down and surrender fully, when we accept our invitation, we will see God undertake in ways we could never have imagined.

As we look into the eyes of those people He places before us, we will have all we need to minister to the whole person. In that moment, we will know what is needed and Holy Spirit will equip us to deal with it through the mighty power of the name of Jesus.

Doing Greater Things Than Jesus Did

There is one promise that the Bible gives us, yet since living my life as a believer, I have seen little evidence of this promise being fulfilled. John 14:12 says,

> *"Very truly I tell you, whoever believes in me will do the works I have been doing, and they will do even greater things than these, because I am going to the Father."*

I do, however, believe the Bible to be the infallible Word of God and, with that in mind believe that this promise, Jesus made will come to pass. Some scholars believe that this scripture has been fulfilled, in as much as disciples of Jesus throughout time have reached many, many more people with the gospel message, than Jesus ever could do in His short three years of ministry on the earth. I do agree, this is very true, but I also believe that Jesus meant that we would do greater things then He did in other areas of ministry also. I believe He was including miracles, healings, and other supernatural occurrences in this statement. As a spirit-filled disciple of Jesus, I feel there is much more to come in these end days. As we submit to serve Him totally and completely, God will use us as His hands and feet on this earth.

We have moved into a new era and the spiritual atmosphere is changing. I believe a time is coming, where the people of God will be challenged to step up. Their commitments and priorities will be challenged. They will no longer just be Sunday Christians, who say all the right things in church on Sunday, but, on Monday they live lives that are not honouring to God. God is shaking and sifting His Church and unfortunately some will fall through the sieve. I don't know what will happen to those people. I don't know if God will class them as those who have fallen away as it talks about in Matthew 24:10:

> *"At that time many will turn away from the faith and will betray and hate one each other".*

1 Timothy 4:1 says,

> *"But the Spirit clearly says that in later times some will abandon the faith, and follow deceiving spirits and things taught by demons".*

I don't know what it means for those people. Those words 'falling away', seem to me to mean just what they say: they will fall away from Jesus, from their faith in Him, from salvation itself maybe? There is a strong possibility that they will be left behind at the rapture of the Church. As I have said before, I am not a theologian, and I am not totally sure of where I stand in relation to the rapture of the church and when that will occur. I sway between pre and mid tribulation. Many will argue with me here and say that once you are saved there is no way you can lose your salvation. Maybe not, I'm not sure. I do believe, however, that some who profess to be Christians will be left behind and will then have to navigate life through the tribulation. I discussed earlier in this book that I believe salvation to be a process. None of us are fully saved until the day Jesus returns and takes His bride home. If we fall away somewhere along the journey of salvation, I believe we may be left behind. It reminds me of Moses. Who would have believed that he would not enter the promised land!

Several years ago, I was battling with this theology of 'once saved, always saved'. I could not reconcile it in my heart. I could not accept that someone could call themselves a Christian just because they had prayed a prayer in a meeting. I don't believe that someone is saved just because they pray a prayer of salvation. Someone can pray that prayer and, the following day continue to live their life with no changes and no transformation. Their life is no different from how it was previously, and they are quite happy to remain in the old lifestyle. Surely, they will not be saved on that final day? Or another example: someone calls themself a Christian because they prayed a prayer of salvation, and went to church regularly. They were involved in ministry but then deny Jesus. Surely this cannot be? God is not one to be mocked. The Bible tells us that He is a jealous God. I don't believe He can overlook sin. He is a holy God; He can neither tolerate sin nor excuse it. He will not turn a blind eye and overlook these things. There has to be a life change, some sort of transformation, some outworking of God in and through a person's life. There must be an ongoing daily repentance.

I was disturbed by this battle going on in my head and I went to bed one night, and prayed. I asked God to show me the truth. Around 3am I woke up, and I couldn't get back to sleep, which very unusual for me. I went downstairs - this was probably the first time I had ever done this. I turned on the TV and put on GOD TV, which I never usually watched. A man was preaching, he was reading from the book of Hebrews 6:4-6:

> *"It is impossible for those who have once been enlightened, who have tasted the heavenly gift, who have shared in the Holy Spirit, who have tasted the goodness of the word of God and the powers of the coming age and who have fallen away, to be brought back to repentance. To their loss they are crucifying the Son of God all over again and subjecting Him to public disgrace."*

I knew in an instant that God was showing me the truth. I do believe that, once we are saved, it is possible to fall away and to miss the rapture if we do not live in obedience to God and live righteous lives through the power of Holy Spirit. In all of this I also know that our God is a God of love and of grace and He wishes that non should perish. We have to balance our disobedience and failings with His love and grace. We need to remember that God sees our hearts and knows our motives. If we are struggling in a particular area and yet our heart is to live a life that honours God, and we are prepared to work with Holy Spirit to put things right, we can be assured that God loves us and He understands. If we persevere and do not give up, we will overcome. He is a gracious and loving God.

During this shaking and sifting of the Church, God is putting out invitations to His people to step up. He is calling His Church out, separating us from the World. Those who choose to say YES to God in these days are the ones who will do greater things than Jesus did. These are the ones that will receive a fresh anointing. Those who refuse this call are, I believe, in a dangerous place. If they choose to live with one foot in the world and one foot in the Kingdom, they are in danger of being amongst those who will fall away in the last days. They are taking a great risk by not separating themselves from the world now.

Those who accept the invitation from the Lord to be separate, to stand, to be purified and to go deeper and higher with Him, who do not fall through the sieve, these are the ones who will see and do greater things than Jesus did. Do you want to be amongst that number? Then you must respond and say 'yes' to your invitation.

What Exactly Did Jesus Do?

Let us look at some of the things that Jesus did, and think about what these greater things might be.

- Jesus declared the good news of the Kingdom of God. Luke 4:43:

> *"But he said to them: "I must declare the good news of the Kingdom of God to other towns also, because that is why I was sent."*

He preached the good news that God would establish His kingdom. In this instance we have already done greater things than Jesus. The Gospel HAS been preached all around the world, and many more people have heard the gospel message and been saved than when Jesus was here.

- Jesus taught Truth.

Jesus taught the people practical lessons about life and how to live a good life. For example, Matthew 6:14 says,

> *"For if you forgive other people when they sin against you, your heavenly Father will also forgive you."*

Matthew 6:34 reads,

> *"Therefore, do not worry about tomorrow, for tomorrow will worry about itself. Each day has enough trouble of its own."*

Again, in relation to teaching or discipleship training in Christian living, many more people have been taught the truth of living lives according to the teachings of the Bible than Jesus Himself could teach while He was here on the earth. We could say here that disciples through the years, have done greater things than Jesus himself did.

- Jesus worked Miracles

John 2:7-10 says,

> *"Jesus said to the servants, "Fill the jars with water"; so, they filled them to the brim. Then he told them, "Now draw some out and take it to the master of the banquet." They did so, and*

> *the master of the banquet tasted the water that had been turned into wine. He did not realize where it had come from, though the servants who had drawn the water knew. Then he called the bridegroom aside and said, "Everyone brings out the choice wine first and then the cheaper wine after the guests have had too much to drink; but you have saved the best till now."*

Here we read of Jesus first miracle. I have, over the years, heard many stories of miracles, for example, people being transported from one place to another with no time lapse and people being made invisible in times of danger, and other such things. But we don't hear of these things every day. However, I do believe many more miracles occur every day, but we fail to acknowledge them as workings of God. We often look at these things as coincidence or just take them for granted, failing to recognise God at work and failing to give God the glory.

That said, I do believe we are going to see many more miracles as the days grow darker, as living life as a Christian becomes more difficult, due to persecution and other troubles. We will need God more than we have ever needed Him before and He will not let us down. We will see Him working in amazing and wondrous ways, as we call on His name in our darkest hours. We must acknowledge Him in all things and give Him all the glory that is due His holy name.

- Jesus Healed the Sick.

Matthew 14:14 reads,

> *"When Jesus landed and saw a large crowd, he had compassion for them and healed their sick".*

Matthew 14:36 says,

> *"...and begged Him to let the sick just touch the edge of His cloak, and all who touched it were healed."*

Matthew 15:30 reads,

> *"Great crowds came to Him, bringing the lame, the blind, the crippled, the mute and many others, and laid them at His feet; and He healed them."*

We read so many stories in the gospels of Jesus healing sick people - blind eyes opened, deaf ears opened, shrivelled limbs growing and even raising people from the dead. The Bible tells us that Jesus healed ALL their diseases. I believe we will see more of this over the coming years. There are very many stories that we hear of modern-day healings. Heidi Baker and her husband Rolland have an incredible work in Mozambique. Their work has had a massive impact on my Christian journey. Faithful servants of Jesus going out and reaching those the world has forgotten. Their work has inspired my husband Ali and I over the years as we have been involved in overseas mission work. I do believe we will see an increase in miraculous healings as we move forward in obedience in these end days, both to reveal the greatness of God to the world and also for believers. The time will come when medical assistance will no longer be available to us because of our faith and love for Jesus.

- Jesus cast out demons

Matthew 8:16 says,

> *"When evening came, many who were demon-possessed were brought to Him, and He drove out the spirits with a word and healed all the sick."*

Jesus cast out demons. He spoke, and they had to leave. Again, as the day draws near, we will see much more of this, many more people will be released and set free from demonic powers and influences in an instant. As we learn to stand in our authority as disciples of Jesus, demons will flee. It doesn't need to be loud and there doesn't need to be any drama. The power of God will be at work and we will be amazed as we start to see many more captives set free.

Why now? What has changed?

We are living in the end-of-the-end days and Jesus is coming very soon for His Bride. We have moved into a new era. This new era arrived during 2020. There was much talk at the beginning of 2020 about clear vision, new vision, 2020 vision. That was so true. As we moved forward into 2020 praying for this 2020 vision, the Lord started to shake the world like never before.

COVID-19 became headline news. The World Health Organisation declared the outbreak as a Public Health concern on 30th January 2020 and declared it a pandemic on 11th March 2020. Cities and countries around the world were locked down, people were restricted in their movements, we were not allowed to leave home, we had to wear face masks, and keep two metres away from other people. Hands – Face – Space became common language. We couldn't visit families, we could not hug our loved ones, we had to isolate in our homes. Self-isolation became common language. Churches were closed, services moved online. We couldn't simply make a Doctor's appointment anymore, we couldn't travel, weddings were cancelled, funerals were restricted. We couldn't visit our sick or even dying relatives in hospital and it goes on. Our freedom was taken from us overnight. Fear took hold and many people became afraid to leave their homes. Even as restrictions have now been lifted many continue to live in fear and stay home. They won't visit shops; they no longer attend church and don't socialise with their friends. Many people are now living in a state of fear that we, in the West have not experienced for over a hundred years.

Alongside Covid, other crazy things were happening in the world. January 2020 saw one of the biggest natural disasters ever seen in Australia as bushfires consumed the country. 18.6 million hectares and over 5,900 buildings were destroyed. Swarms of locusts in Africa and Asia, fires, floods, volcanic eruptions, earthquakes and the list went on. In August 2021, the US president removed American troops from Afghanistan after 20 years of peace keeping, Afghanistan is now totally controlled by the Taliban. Horrendous atrocities are happening there, and we hear more and more stories every day. Women and girls being hunted down and abused, and Christians being murdered. The whole climate change agenda is now being rammed down our throats and, if we disagree, we are somehow a lesser class citizen.

The LGBTQ+ agenda has also infiltrated our whole society, Children are being taught in school that they can choose if they want to be male or female, regardless of their biological makeup. None of this is biblical. Even science tells us we are born either male or female, it is a physical thing. You can try and make scripture fit and say what you want it to say. You can find scriptures to legitimise what is now culturally accepted and expected of everyone. Churches are trying to fit in to the worldly agenda to modernise and be culturally relevant, but we cannot change what the Bible says. The Church is supposed to stand out, be different, set a godly example. It is getting harder and harder to speak godly, biblical truth without being called a bigot, a racist, a chauvinist, homophobic, brainwashed, or a multitude of other labels. Governments around the world are now trying to criminalise praying for people in regard to their sexuality and to preach truth on the streets. If we preach truth we are seen as inciting hatred. It is now known as a hate crime.

I recently read a newsletter 'End Times Bible Prophecy' by Britt Gillette entitled "Are we on the verge of the tribulation?" (see Appendix). Much of what I read I was already aware of but to read it and digest it in this format, confirmed to me that we are most certainly living in the end-of-the-end days.

As Christians we should not be surprised by any of this, for it is written in the Bible that these things will happen. Unfortunately, it is only going to get darker. We are in a new era, the end-of-the-end days. Jesus is coming very soon for His purified Bride. As the days get darker, we will burn brighter. We need to be sanctified and purified in order for His light to burn bright within us. We will do greater things than Jesus did in the dark days that lie ahead.

We have a choice to make. We need to accept the invitation that is there for all of us to step up, to step out, to be separated, to be holy and righteous, to be obedient and to honour Jesus our Saviour with our all in these days. Are you ready to make that decision yet? If not, then you are going to miss out on so much. He has so much more for you; there is so much more of God available to us. I am receiving regular fresh revelation in these days. Let us remember that God is the Creator and created all things. Let us not leave it too long because the hour is drawing near when Jesus will return. We must be ready.

Absolutely, we will do greater things than Jesus did, but first we must stand up in this final generation.

Revealing The Secrets of His Heart

In this new era, I believe with all my heart that Jesus wants to reveal the secrets of His heart to His children. There is so much that He wants to say to us in these last days. He has tender loving things to say. He has encouragements to bring. He has hard to-hear chastisements to deliver. He has missions to reveal. He has direction to give. He has blueprints and strategies to download. He has pictures to paint, and visions to unravel. There is so much on His heart in these days that He wants to download to the hearts of His people. Are you open for that, are you ready to receive? Even if it's not what you may have been expecting or hoping for? Even if it is more difficult than you may have anticipated and requires sacrifices to be made?

What stops us from hearing?

There are a few things that may stop us from receiving the secrets of God's heart. As I mention a few things here, see if anything that I am saying resonates with you. I do believe that there is at least one reason why God may stop speaking to us and that is disobedience. However, most of the time He is speaking, we either don't hear Him or don't recognise His voice.

We are not ready to receive His secrets

Are you ready to listen? Are you ready to receive? Are you ready to live in obedience? Let us remember God already knows our heart and He knows if we will obey Him. So, if you are waiting to hear from Him, if you are expecting Him to reveal the secrets of His heart to you, yet you are not totally laid down and have not died to yourself, you may miss what He is saying. He may not speak if your heart is not ready to receive or if you are disobedient. Jesus sees our hearts, every nook and cranny. He knows us better than we know ourselves. If we want God to reveal His secrets to us, we need to be ready to receive and to respond.

Too busy, too noisy.

Sometimes our lives are so busy and full of noise that we cannot hear what God is saying. I believe that God is speaking to us all the time, but too often we are not tuned in to Him. We have filled our lives with noise. This means it is impossible to hear the voice of God. Many of us have busy lives but we should never be too busy for God. He should be priority before anything or anyone else. Does listening to God take priority over everything else in our lives? If not, we need to make some changes, make space and quieten the noise so that we can hear Him.

We can be busy with God things, and we can be busy with good things. Let us stop for a second and think about the things that fill our time each day; are they really God things? There may even be some things that we do that are actually not good! If you are too busy and don't have time for God, something must go. Obviously, the things that are not good should be at the top of the list to be cut out, but also some of the good things may need to go too. It is possible that some of the good things we do are things that God never asked or intended for us to do in the first place. Seek the Lord and ask Him what needs to go. If you're anything like me you want to help and do things for other people. You want to be involved in serving at Church, because you are a servant and a doer. This is not a bad thing in itself, but if you are one of these people, it is very easy to say 'yes' to things that God never asked you to do, because you want to help and please people.

Many years ago, a friend said to me, "Lorraine, do you know that 'No' is an anointed word, you don't have to say 'yes' to everything?" That word from a friend set me free. I realised that just because I was being asked to help, it didn't mean that I should. I sometimes needed to say 'no'. I needed to ask God what I was to say 'yes' to. I don't do anything now unless I know that it is something the Lord has said I should do.

Stop for a moment and ask the Lord what things you need to stop doing.

Disobedience

It may be that you are not hearing from the Lord because of disobedience in your life. He may have asked you to do something previously and you didn't do it. If we don't do the things the Lord requires or asks of us, He may stop speaking to us. He may call someone else to do what He had intended for us to do. Let us be sure to live in obedience and do the things the Lord is asking us to do. Remember the scripture in Luke 16:10:

> *"Whoever can be trusted with very little can also be trusted with much"*

Let us not miss out on the exciting things the Lord has for us because we are not walking in obedience to Him.

Sin

Is there some sin in your life that is separating you from the Lord? If there is sin, we are not living in a right relationship with God. The longer it goes on, the further away from Him we move. The further away from God we are, the harder it is for us to hear what He is saying. It's the same in the natural. If you are in the same room, it is easy to hear someone speaking to you, but if you go upstairs, even if they shout, you may not hear. Unrepented sin may be the reason you no longer hear the voice of the Lord. You have moved away, into another room, and sin has placed a barrier between you and God. Let us remember that it is us who move away from God; He does not move away from us. God is still there, He still loves us and is still speaking but we have positioned ourselves far away from Him due to our sinful actions, attitudes, or desires.

Let us check our hearts and ask Holy Spirit to reveal any sin that may be separating us from Jesus? He is only a prayer away. Turn around and take that first step of repositioning yourself. Repent and ask for forgiveness, turn around and start walking home. His arms are wide open waiting for you. You will very soon start to hear His voice again as you move closer to Him.

God has an assignment for you

Time is short and Jesus is returning very soon for His spotless Bride. Our primary task is to ensure we are ready and then we should make sure we are doing everything we can to help others to prepare themselves.

God has a plan and a purpose for you. There is a reason that you are alive in this moment. God has an assignment just for you. Do you know what your assignment is? You need to seek His face like never before and ask the Lord to reveal His heart to you in this moment in eternity. We need to align ourselves ready for His plans to be released into our hearts. Are you sensing the urgency of the times that we are living in? - Time is short! There are billions of people who do not yet know Jesus; there are many people who think that they do know Jesus but in reality, they are far from Him.

It is time for the Church to leave the building and to get out into the world. Gone are the days of the feel-good church services. It is time to get our hands dirty. We can no longer sit in our comfortable church buildings and let the world carry on as if nothing is happening. The world needs to know what is really going on. Who is going to tell them if we lock ourselves away in our cosy cliques?

It is time for us to stand up, to get our hearts sorted and to get serious about Jesus. Let us find out what assignment He has for us and get on with it. We are living in exciting days! God is moving in unprecedented ways and some Christians still want to get back to 'normal'. Many are going to miss this new wave of Holy Spirit at work because they are stuck in the past and expecting Him to move in the same way as He did before. God is moving and He is at work. Watch and see what He is doing! He is doing a new thing! Don't miss it!

Things to come

We are living in days when God is revealing to His prophets the things that are to come. He is showing them the days ahead. Amos 3:7-8 says,

> *"Surely the Sovereign Lord does nothing without revealing His plan to His servants the prophets."*

Could it be possible that you are one of the people that the Lord has revelation for? Could He have things that He wants to reveal to you, but you are wrongly positioned? Get positioned, get ready, get prepared. You may be one of those He wants to speak to.

Read God's Word and receive revelation

The Bible tells us of things to come and what we should look for in the-end-days. We should not be surprised by any of it. We need to read the Word of God and digest it within our very being so we will not be taken by surprise, so we are ready and prepared for what is to come. The Lord reveals His heart through Scripture. We must read the Scriptures regularly and listen to what He is saying to us in these days.

A time of Greater Sacrifice

I believe we are living in a time of greater revelation, and that God is speaking to many believers, those who are prepared to sacrifice for Him. He is asking more of us in these days. We know in our hearts if we are willing to sacrifice the things of this World for Him. As we recognise the things in our lives that hinder our relationship with Jesus, then we must lay them down. If we have a desire to receive the greater revelations from Him, we have to make sacrifices. It may be alcohol, relationships, certain foods, activities, anything that gets in the way of our relationship with Jesus. We have to lay them down if we want to live our best and fullest life in Him and for Him. If we are not prepared to make these sacrifices, we will still be saved but we will not be the best we can be. We may not receive the fullness of all the good and great plans that He has prepared in advance for us to do on this earth in these days. How far are you prepared to go for Him who gave everything up for you?

Called to be Watchman!

During the first UK coronavirus lockdown in March 2020, I had been praying and listening to God to see what He was wanting to say to me at that time, when a video popped up on my Facebook feed. It was of a man in Indonesia, he was standing on the balcony of a building looking out to sea. There was a road below and then shops, cafes, bars, a beach and then the sea in the distance. The man was shouting to the people below because He could see something that they could not see. He was looking out and could see a big wave coming in; he could see a tsunami! He was shouting and screaming at the people trying to warn them but, either they didn't hear him, they didn't understand him, or they ignored him, because they didn't seem to move until it was too late and the water came crashing in.

As I watched this video, I had a knot in my stomach and God really got my attention, I was reminded in that moment that we have a job to do in these last days. We have a responsibility as Christians; we are called to be watchmen.

What is a Watchman?

In today's society we would probably call them security guards, or we may use the term night watchmen for someone who watches over and protects property or people during the night. In Biblical times, a watchman would normally be found on the city walls, and it was their job to blow the shofar when danger was approaching. They would also be able to see the comings and goings of daily life, the activities on the streets and in the marketplace. They would know the people and their lifestyles. If they were based near the city gates, they would often observe the business of the city officials taking place, as this was where transactions were made. They would also be able to see the arrival of any visitors the city would be receiving. Most importantly they would see the King when he had been away and was returning. They would be able to warn people of the King's return so preparations could be made. Does this sound familiar?

Who are the Watchmen of today?

I believe that we, as Christians, are called to be watchmen, and this is a great responsibility. I don't believe it is solely the responsibility of leaders, but of all us who confess Christ.

In Marks gospel (Mark 13:1-37), Jesus is teaching his disciples concerning the signs that will precede His return. He warns them against spiritual sleepiness. He concludes that teaching in v 37, by saying,

> *"What I say to you, I say to everyone, Watch."*

This says to me that we are part of 'everyone.' He wasn't just speaking to those with Him, He was also speaking to us who are reading His Word today.

As Christians we firstly have a responsibility to watch over our own lives making sure that we are walking in daily repentance and dealing with any issues Holy spirit reveals to us, living in obedience to God. Ephesians 4:27 says:

> *"Do NOT give the devil a foothold" (some translations say opportunity).*

The imagery used here by Paul is one of a steep rock face which is difficult to climb. If we are walking in obedience to God and living righteous lives, our lives are like this smooth rock face and there is no place for the devil to get in. But as soon as we start to entertain any kind of iniquity and we start to waiver off the right path it gives footholds for the devil to gain access; the devil will use every opportunity. Therefore, it is important to keep watch over our own lives first. We should then watch over our families and then we have a responsibility to be watching continually over those whom the Lord places within our sphere of influence.

What are we watching for?

As watchmen there are a number of things that we are watching for as we look out and watch from our vantage point. As Christians we can see things from a different viewpoint, from a different position. We are able to see things that others cannot see. Just like in Bible times they stood in their tower to watch, we are in Christ, who is our strong fortified tower. Proverbs 18:10 reads,

> *"The name of the LORD is a fortified tower, the righteous run into it, and are safe."*

As well as being safe in this tower we are raised up and so can see from a different vantage point. We see from an elevated position in Christ Jesus. So, what are we looking for?

There are at least four things we are to watch for. **"Watch"** is mentioned in 26 books of the Bible and occurs at least 57 **times**, so it's quite a big subject. It's pretty important.

Watching to see if there is anyone in need

Just as the Watchmen of old, on the city wall, could often see human need and be able to send someone to help, from our position in Christ, we can see those who may be in need. This gives us an opportunity to help those people. As we seek God's face, as we watch and pray, He will show us those who need help. We should always have our hearts open and be looking to see what the Lord is seeing. As we see as God sees, we can do as God does. As we see need, we can then do our best to help in any way we can. We may recognise loneliness in someone's heart, we may see grief or pain, we may see a physical need for healing, or it may be a practical or financial need. It may be all we can do is pray, but whatever need we see we should always do something. We should not ignore it; we should respond in some way. If we are not watching, we will not see. We should not shut our eyes to these things, for as Christians, we are called to help orphans, widows, those in poverty, and those hurting and broken. This is part of our mandate, so we must keep our eyes open and keep watch.

Watching to see what God is doing

We are in a position where we can see things from God's perspective, which is often different from the perspective of the World. But we have to watch and pray in order to gain God's perspective and see what He is doing. If we ask questions like, "Lord, what are you doing in our church, or our town, or our country?" He will tell us. We have the awesome privilege as Christians to be able to have a relationship with God. We can talk to him and He responds. Part of all relationships is watching, we watch to see a person's behaviour, or body language. As we watch a person, we get to know them. We learn things about them and it is no different with God. We seek His face and sense His mood and feelings in any given situation. We might not see with our eyes but we will see in our spirit, in our heart. Remember we are one with Christ Jesus and, as we watch and pray into the things He is revealing to us, we will see things clearer from His perspective.

We need to keep watching and praying so that we don't miss anything. When we do start to see something of what God is doing in any given situation, in our church, in a certain geographical location, in someone's life or even in our own life, we should then respond in an appropriate way.

Our response may mean more prayer. We may only have seen [a little,] so we can pray more into that situation. God may want us to share it with others so they can be involved. If we don't watch, we could miss it. Whatever we see we need to respond. God shows us things so as we can partner with Him in what He is doing. In Proverbs 8: 34, there is a lovely scripture that captures a little of what I am trying to say:

> *"Joyful are those who listen to Me, watching for Me daily at My doors, waiting at My doorway!"*

We sit and watch and wait until He reveals the things that are stirring His heart and then we can get involved, in whatever way He asks us to.

Watching for danger from enemy attack

Certainly, in Old Testament times, defensive watchfulness was at the heart of a watchman's work. The watchmen on the wall were always on the alert for any attempt of an enemy to attack or infiltrate the city. Too many times, the walls of the Church are open to attack because of a lack of watchfulness. Unless praying watchmen are on duty, we too often find ourselves painfully unaware of the attempts of the enemy to disrupt and destroy the great work God is doing.

We read in Ezekiel 33 how Ezekiel was called by God to be a watchman over the nation of Israel. His responsibility was to blow the shofar when danger was approaching. Ezekiel 33 talks of two kinds of people - the righteous and the wicked:

> *"Therefore, son of man, say to your people, 'If someone who is righteous disobeys, that person's former righteousness will count for nothing. And if someone who is wicked repents, that person's*

> *former wickedness will not bring condemnation. The righteous person who sins will not be allowed to live even though they were formerly righteous.' If I tell a righteous person that they will surely live, but then they trust in their righteousness and do evil, none of the righteous things that person has done will be remembered; they will die for the evil they have done. And if I say to a wicked person, 'You will surely die,' but they then turn away from their sin and do what is just and right if they give back what they took in pledge for a loan, return what they have stolen, follow the decrees that give life, and do no evil that person will surely live; they will not die. None of the sins that person has committed will be remembered against them. They have done what is just and right; they will surely live."*

From our raised vantage point, we can watch for danger, just like Ezekiel did on the walls. As we see danger drawing near, we can blow the horn and warn those who are in danger, both the righteous and the unrighteous.

The Righteous

Ezekiel 33:12 says,

> *"Therefore, son of man, say to your people, 'If someone who is righteous disobeys, that person's former righteousness will count for nothing".*

We have a responsibility to our brothers and sisters in Christ, to tell them if we see that they are in danger. I am not saying that we have the right to go around the church and start to criticise and drag people down. This is definitely not what I am saying. Over the years I have heard so many sad stories of people who are no longer walking with God because other Christians, Pastors or Leaders have hurt them so badly that they have left the Church. These things need to be dealt with in love and with lots of wisdom. Only if we are sure that God has shown us something very clearly, and only if we have examined ourselves first should we share something. Just a note here, we should all be open to listen if a brother or sister in Christ, who we know and respect, comes to us and tells us something about what they have seen regarding us or our life. We should not be defensive. We should go away and, as a mature Christian, take it to the Lord and test it. If it is shown to be true, then we need to deal with it. If not then we need to lay it down. This takes a much deeper level of spiritual maturity.

Let us look at Matthew 7:1-6 where this is dealt with:

> *"Do not judge, or you too will be judged. For in the same way you judge others, you will be judged, and with the measure you use, it will be measured to you."*

The Message paraphrases it like this, "Don't pick on people, jump on their failures, criticize their faults - unless, of course, you want the same treatment."

This is, to me, much clearer. Unless we are prepared to undergo the same treatment, and unless we are open for others to point out to us our weaknesses or failures, then we should certainly not be doing it. Like I said earlier, this needs a deep level of Christian spiritual maturity. Matthew 7:3-5 says:

> *"Why do you look at the speck of sawdust in your brother's eye and pay no attention to the plank in your own eye? How can you say to your brother, 'Let me take the speck out of your eye,' when all the time there is a plank in your own eye? You hypocrite, first take the plank out of your own eye, and then you will see clearly to remove the speck from your brother's eye."*

We are not prohibited from discerning sin or problems in our Christian brother or sister, but we must first examine ourselves to make sure nothing in us prevents us from seeing clearly in that situation. Then, and only then, says Jesus, you can "see clearly to remove the speck from your brother's eye", always remembering we should only operate out of a heart of love for the other person.

We need to be real, authentic watchmen with a much deeper level of Christian maturity as we watch over those inside the walls.

The Unrighteous

As Christians we have a responsibility to watch over those who are unsaved. We need to warn them of the coming judgment of God and that, unless they repent and turn back to God, they are in a dangerous place. We, as Christians, have a responsibility to share the way of Jesus with those the Lord places before us. It is our responsibility to tell them the truth, to tell them about Jesus who died for them, to tell them that there is another way, a way of righteousness, and that they need to turn away from their life of sin and turn towards God who loves them, before it is too late. They need to know that there is a way to eternity with God. How will they know if we do not tell them? As we watch, and God shows us these people, we need to tell them the truth. God loves the world so much He sent Jesus to die, how can we keep this good news to ourselves?

We must remember that people in the world watch the Church. They will be very quick to point out if we are being hypocritical, I'm not saying we need to be living a perfect Christian life, though we do need to be seen to be living an authentic Christian life, and operating in love and not judgment, otherwise we make a mockery of the Church.

Watching for the Bridegroom

Jesus is coming back for His Church very soon, and we need to watch for Him. We can do this by being aware of the signs of the times we are living in.

1 Chronicles 12:32 says, in the NLT,

> *"From the tribe of Issachar, there were 200 leaders of the tribe with their relatives. All these men understood the signs of the times and knew the best course for Israel to take."*

In Amos 3:7, we read:

> *"Surely the Sovereign LORD does nothing without revealing his plan to his servants the prophets."*

In Luke 12:54-56, Luke records how Jesus rebuked the crowds,

> *He said to the crowd: "When you see a cloud rising in the west, immediately you say, 'It's going to rain,' and it does. And when the south wind blows, you say, 'It's going to be hot,' and it is. Hypocrites! You know how to interpret the appearance of the earth and the sky. How is it that you don't know how to interpret this present time?*

In Matthew 24 and Luke 21, you can read detailed teaching concerning the end times. Please read these passages and see what Jesus says about the signs of the end days and compare them what is happening today.

We need to be aware of the signs of the times we are living in and we need to be watching for the Bridegroom. We need to be like the men of Issachar who understood the signs of the times. Remember that the sovereign Lord does nothing without first revealing His plans to His servants, the prophets. We need to be watching, listening and preparing for Jesus' return. If we neglect to watch and pray how can God reveal these things to us? How will we see, how will we be ready?

Remember the warning Jesus gave when he told the story of the 10 virgins; 5 were ready and 5 were not. You can read this in Luke 12:35-40.

Joel 2:1 says,

> *"Blow the trumpet in Zion; sound the alarm on My holy hill. Let all who live in the land tremble, for the day of the LORD is coming. It is close at hand"z*

We the watchmen, are to be those who sound the trumpet from our raised vantage point in Jesus Christ. So let the sound go out and give the warning, so that people will be ready and not be taken unaware.

God will reveal the secrets of His heart in these end-of-the-end days, if we are watching and waiting to hear what He has to say. We then need to Stand up and do the things He is calling us to do, in this final generation. Will the final generation please stand?

Time to Grow Up?

The Bible talks a lot about spiritual maturity. This chapter is a call to maturity. We have been babies in Jesus for far too long and now it is time to grow up.

Ephesians 4:11-16 says:

> *"So, Christ himself gave the apostles, the prophets, the evangelists, the pastors, and teachers, to equip his people for works of service, so that the body of Christ may be built up until we all reach unity in the faith and in the knowledge of the Son of God and become mature, attaining to the whole measure of the fullness of Christ. Then we will no longer be infants, tossed back and forth by the waves, and blown here and there by every wind of teaching and by the cunning and craftiness of people in their deceitful scheming. Instead, speaking the truth in love, we will grow to become in every respect the mature body of him who is the head, that is, Christ. From him the whole body, joined and held together by every supporting ligament, grows, and builds itself up in love, as each part does its work".*

It says in this verse in Ephesians that Christ gave the Church apostles, prophets, evangelists, pastors, and teachers. He gave the fivefold ministry gifts so we would be fully equipped to become true servants of God, so that we may reach a unity in our faith and become mature in Christ Jesus attaining the fullness of God. It goes on to say that once we are mature, we will no longer be infants who are tossed around by the waves, blown here, there and everywhere with every wind of teaching. It will be more difficult for us to be deceived. Once we are mature Christians and have reached our fullness in Christ, we can find our right place of service, in the body of Christ. We will join with other parts of the body supporting and encouraging each other, building up the whole body together as we each do our appointed work.

Have you found your place yet?

Have you found your place yet, or are you still drinking milk from your church pastors and teachers, yearning for that prophecy to set you on your life track or to give you direction? Whether we are relatively new Christians or have been Christians for a long time, it is critical that we wean ourselves off the milk that we receive from our Church leaders. Of course, we all need to start somewhere and, when we are new Christians, we need guidance and reassurance, encouraging and building up. I feel that generally most of us stay in that place for far too long. This isn't always our fault, sometimes our pastors and leaders don't encourage us as they should to stand on our own two feet and find our place. As I have said many times in these pages, time is short, Jesus is coming back very soon, and we have a lot of work to do. We will not find our position, or appointed role in God's Church by sitting Sunday after Sunday listening to preachers, singing worship songs and having a nice fun time with our Church friends. It will, of course, be of great benefit to us, providing we are being taught sound biblical truths, though we do need to act on the things we are hearing. That said, once a week on a Sunday attending church listening to a sermon and having half an hour of worship is not enough. We need so much more than this.

Are you a Giver or are you a Taker?

Are you a servant of Jesus? Are you working out your salvation?

Or, do you just sit back and enjoy the ride, allowing your leaders or other Christian friends to do all the work for you?

A turning point for me in my Christian walk came one Sunday. I had been to church as usual, and I felt that I hadn't received anything at all from the service. I am sure I'm not alone here. Have you ever been to church and thought, 'I should have stayed at home and had a lie in, that service did nothing for me?' Well, this particular Sunday, that is how I was thinking and feeling. The preaching went right over my head, the worship did not lift my spirits. I was bored and fed up, and I was whining to myself about how bad the service had been. Out of nowhere, this Bible verse came into my mind. "Jesus came to serve not to be served." (Matthew 20:28) In that instant something changed within me, and I vowed I would never complain about a church service again. Instead, I would get on board and get involved. The very next week I was serving coffees, and I have been serving in church and other Christian ministry ever since. That one line of scripture changed me forever.

Activate Holy Spirit

When you are born again, the Spirit of God comes to reside within you. We know this, but has the Spirit of God been activated within you? Do you operate in the things of the Spirit?

How do we activate Holy Spirit? It is not really very complicated, we ask Him to consume us. We pray and talk to Him and ask Him to work in us and through us. We give Him permission to clean up any mess that He might find. It is important that as Christians we work in partnership with the Spirit of God. He brings along with Him many gifts; the Bible tells us that we have all we need within us to live godly lives. We just need to learn to walk with Him; we need to be obedient. We need to deal with any sin issues that He may reveal. If you have a lifestyle that goes against God, then stop it. If it's hard then ask Holy Spirit to help. Believe that He is there to help you, to enable you to live a godly life. We should not live defeated lives as Christians; we are called to be overcomers. Jesus came so that we may have life and life to the full.

Read the Word of God regularly

Isn't it incredible how scripture can change us. Our thoughts, attitudes, character, and our actions can all be changed in an instant. Why are we surprised? Isn't that the purpose of scripture? That is why we need to read it regularly. The bible tells us in 2 Timothy 3:16-17:

> *"All scripture is God breathed and is useful for teaching, rebuking, correcting, and training in righteousness, so that the servant of God may be thoroughly equipped for every good work".*

It is vitally important, if we want to mature in our walk with the Lord, that we regularly read our Bible. I fully understand that it is not always easy. It is sometimes the most difficult thing in the world to find time in a day to read God's Word. I can assure you that the more you do it, the easier it becomes. Here are a few ideas that may help:

- It may seem hard to read and you feel like you are treading through treacle; it may seem like it is just words on a page. It is true, sometimes the Bible is difficult to understand. Find a version that is easier for you. There are many different translations and paraphrases of the Bible and sometimes it helps to read a translation like The Good News Bible or a paraphrased version like the Living Bible. Try a few different ones and see which you are more comfortable with.
- Always pray before you read your Bible and ask God to give you revelation and understanding. You will be amazed at how that can help.
- Find a place in the house where it is quiet, and you will not be disturbed. Tell the family that you will be busy for the next half hour or so and they shouldn't disturb you unless

it's an emergency. Let them know that it is an important time for you.
- Find a time that works best for you. Try and get into a routine and stick to it.
- Don't be hard on yourself if you miss a day. Don't be religious about it. If you don't get a chance or something happens then try again tomorrow. Tomorrow is always a new day.
- Be aware that, anytime you set aside to read God's Word, there will be distractions and it will not be easy. Your enemy the devil is desperate that you don't read the Bible and he will do all he can to distract and disturb you. If you do manage to find time and space, be assured he will infiltrate your mind and fill your thoughts with other things. Persevere, don't give up. Pray and ask God to clear your head from the distractions and try again.

I promise it does get easier. It has taken me years to get to a place where I have a regular quiet time, I would be lying if I said it was every day because things still get in the way of my time with the Lord. But I know how important it is for me if I want to be in the right place with my Jesus, if I want to keep in tune with Him, if I want to hear His voice. It is critical for my walk with Him that I make space for Him. This does come with maturity and can take some time. But don't give up, keep going and you will, one day, cherish the times you spend each day with Jesus.

Develop your Prayer Life

As we become more mature as Christian's, prayer becomes part of our life. It becomes easier and more natural, and you find yourself talking to God in all situations and on all occasions, and this is what it should be like.

At first it may feel awkward, but Jesus is your friend. He wants a relationship with you, and you can't get to know someone if you don't talk to them. Be open and honest with Him, tell Him how you're feeling, good and bad; say thank you for all that He has done and air your disappointment in the areas you may be struggling. Incorporate prayer with your Bible reading, talk to Him as you read and ask Him to explain the words you are reading. If you are having a bad day, give thanks to God. Think about the good things in your life, even in the worst of situations. On the darkest of days, you can usually find something good to give thanks for. You will be surprised how it lifts your spirit and changes your perspective. The more you pray, the easier it becomes. It is like reading your Bible, the more you do it, the more it becomes part of who you are.

Meet with other Christians

Try to build relationships with other Christians and spend time with them. Talk about your faith and the things you may be struggling with. Talk about what excites you. Talk about the dreams and visions God has given you. It is also good to talk about what you have read in the Bible. If there is a passage you have struggled with understanding, ask your friends what they think. Also pray with your friends; this may be hard at first and seem strange. You will get used to it and it will become a natural part of your relationship with your Christian friends. You will pray with each other and for each other, encouraging each other and building one another up.

Be a Servant

I wrote earlier and asked if you were a servant. This is so important. It is all well and good, reading our Bibles and praying and meeting with our Christian friends, but if we are not serving then why are we even bothering with any of these other things? You will find that the more you get to know Jesus the more you will want to serve Him.

Christian maturity is about being more like Jesus today than you were yesterday. If you are not serving you are not like Jesus. Jesus was a servant King! We should be servants of our Lord Jesus Christ;

this should be the most natural thing in the world. He loves us, He died for us, we love Him and we are thankful for what He has done for us. Naturally we want to serve Him, we want to do the things that he asks us to do.

You may not know where to start. If that is you, ask Jesus to give you vision and direction. Tell Him you want to be His servant and ask Him what He wants you to do for Him. You will be amazed how things will start to change and how doors of opportunity will open. Believe me, the more you serve, the more opportunities you will get. If you don't feel you are sure of what God is asking of you, just serve anyway. Ask at your church if there is anything you can do to help. You will find the more you do, the more you want to do. Just do something!

Spiritual maturity is a process and takes time, It depends how much we want it. Do you have a desperation within you to be more like Jesus every day? With the help of the Spirit of God you can be more like Jesus day by day. Each day you can grow from one degree of glory to another. This is what the bible tells us should be happening as we walk with Jesus. 2 Corinthians 3:18 tells us this,

> *"And all of us, with unveiled faces, seeing the glory of the Lord as though reflected in a mirror, are being transformed into the same image from one degree of glory to another, for this comes from the Lord, the Spirit". (NRSV)*

Stop relying on your pastor or leaders, or other Christians. Grow up, dig deep and plant your roots deep in faith. Stand on God's word, step out and walk in obedience to the things He is calling you to. Be established in Him and you will be mature, and will be able to stand in this final generation.

A way to Maturity, To Obey is better than Sacrifice

In February 2021, I woke up one night with a scripture from 1

Samuel 15 flying round in my head. In 1 Samuel 15, God commands Saul to go and destroy the Amalekite nation and spare no life. So Saul went and destroyed the Amalekites just as God had told him to. He captured King, Agag, but Saul's army also kept the best of the sheep, goats and cattle. In the night, however, God woke up Samuel and said in v 11: "I am sorry I ever made Saul King, for he has not been loyal to me and has refused to obey my command." In the morning Samuel went to find Saul to challenge him on what God had said. Samuel found Saul, who was very happy with himself. Saul said to Samuel, "May the Lord bless you; I have carried out the Lord's command!" Samuel's response was not as positive; "If that is the case what are all these animals". Saul then went on to justify His actions by saying that they kept the best of the livestock so they could sacrifice them to the Lord.

1 Samuel 15 v 16 – 25:

> *"Enough!" Samuel said to Saul. "Let me tell you what the Lord said to me last night." "Tell me," Saul replied. Samuel said, "Although you were once small in your own eyes, did you not become the head of the tribes of Israel? The Lord anointed you king over Israel. And he sent you on a mission, saying, 'Go and completely destroy those wicked people, the Amalekites; wage war against them until you have wiped them out.' Why did you not obey the Lord? Why did you pounce on the plunder and do evil in the eyes of the Lord?" "But I did obey the Lord," Saul said. "I went on the mission the Lord assigned me. I completely destroyed the Amalekites and brought back Agag their king. The soldiers took sheep and cattle from the plunder, the best of what was devoted to God, in order to sacrifice them to the Lord your God at Gilgal." But Samuel replied: "Does the Lord delight in burnt offerings and sacrifices as much as in obeying the Lord? To obey is better than sacrifice, and to heed is better than the fat of rams. For rebellion is like the sin of divination, and arrogance like the evil of idolatry. Because you have rejected the word of the Lord, he has rejected you as king." Then Saul*

> *said to Samuel, "I have sinned. I violated the Lord's command and your instructions. I was afraid of the men and so I gave in to them. Now I beg you, forgive my sin and come back with me, so that I may worship the Lord."*

The part of the scripture that I had in my head was from v22:

"Obedience is better than sacrifice".

What a picture this story paints; we have a proud Saul who thinks he has done a good job, but in reality, he did not obey God, he partly obeyed, he thought he had done enough. He probably did 99% of what he was told to do. But, unfortunately, being partly obedient is being disobedient. God called it rebellion; He then said it is like the sin of divination. Some translations say, 'rebellion is as witchcraft.' The first time I read this scripture it really caught my attention, and I made the decision that I always had to do as God asked, that I could never ignore His commands. It was a shock to me to think that if I didnt obey God it was as bad as being involved in occult practices. I remember my mum once saying to me, I think it was in relation to us going to Africa, she said, *"You don't always have to say yes to God, you Know."* I replied, "I'm sorry Mum but yes, I do; I always have to be obedient and do what God calls me to do."

We cannot be a little bit obedient; we are either obedient or disobedient and if we are disobedient, we are rebelling against God. The Bible tells us that rebellion is as witchcraft or as bad as being involved in occult practices (The Message).

Some of us would probably say about Saul, "It's OK, he did his best." We may even defend Saul and say, "Give him credit for what he did do, why point out the one thing he didn't do." "Don't be so hard on him."

But at the end of the day Saul was disobedient to God.

What did Saul actually do?

Saul told Samuel that he had taken the best livestock to offer as a sacrifice to God. Saul used sacrifice as an excuse for his disobedience. He used it to justify his shortcomings.

Is it possible that some of us Christians do the same? We do good things, we help the poor and give to charity, we serve in church, we attend all the prayer meetings, we fast and pray we do all the spiritual stuff, BUT, unfortunately, sometimes we have wrong motives. We can be doing all these good things, but deep down we know that there is one thing we are not doing, that God has asked us to do.

In Matthew 6, Jesus criticized the teachers for similar practices. He noted three religious' activities - fasting, public prayer, and giving to those in need. These activities were often used to look good in front of other people, rather than to honour God. As with Saul, the problem was not the offerings. It was not a problem that the Pharisees were doing these things, the problem was the reason why they were doing what they are doing; they were desiring the approval of people rather than the approval of God.

Matthew 22:37-39, often related to as the greatest commandment, says,

> *Jesus replied, "Love the Lord your God with all your heart and with all your soul and with all your mind." This is the first and greatest commandment. And the second is like it: "Love your neighbour as yourself."*

Why do we do the things we do?

Is it because, like the Pharisees, we want to look good in front of others? Does it make us feel good? Or, is it because we feel we have a duty to do it because we are Christians and that's what Christians do? If we are doing anything for any reason other than because of our love for God, all we are doing is making unnecessary sacrifices. Right, godly sacrifices come out of obedience to Him, not just to make us look good, or even to make us feel better.

When you truly love someone, you will do anything for that person, for no other reason than because you love them. If we truly love God with all our hearts and with all our souls and with all our minds, it should not be difficult to obey Him.

He is a good God. He loves us, He cares for us, He wants the best for us and He sees the beginning from the end. God desires obedience not because he is threatened by our actions or our will, but because our obedience is best for us. He wants the best for us.

When God tells us to do something, we should not hesitate in being obedient. We should not even need to think about it, we should just do it, immediately.

Has He told you to do something? Are you are being disobedient? You're thinking about it, you're procrastinating and doing other things first, because they are good things to do, but maybe God hasn't asked you to do those things. Do you know deep down within that something is not right in your life, that you have issues going on that need to be sorted and you keep putting it off. Don't wait a minute longer, just do it, put it right, be obedient, do it now.

We can go to as many meetings as we like and make as many sacrifices as we want to, give as much money away as we can and help everyone who asks, but if we are not being obedient to whatever it is that God is asking of us, then it is all in vain. Everything we do, however good it might be, is pointless.

Sometimes we try to justify not doing the one thing He has asked of us by keeping ourselves busy doing all these other things, making all these sacrifices for Him. But we must remember that disobedience is rebellion against God, and He says rebellion is as witchcraft.

Why might we be disobedient?

There are many reasons why we might be disobedient to God. A few reasons are fear, pride, selfishness, pressure from others. The fear of man was Saul's excuse, *"I was afraid of the men and so I gave in to them"*.

God may be asking you to do something and you're not doing it because you think it might upset someone. This is often a reason why we don't do what God is asking of us. With the best will in the world as you try to protect others, if your being disobedient, it will not have the best outcome. God sees the end, He calls us for good reason, for a purpose, because He wants the best for us.

An example from my own life: When God spoke to Ali and I about going to Africa, there were members of our family who didn't want us to go for various reasons and they were upset when we went, but if we hadn't gone when God told us to, we would have been disobeying Him by putting our family first. Now that's a tough one! We should not put anyone or anything before God, He should come first in all things, before anything and everything, before our own desires, before our family. God should be first. Above all else.

There are two types of obedience; there is a general obedience to follow God's commands and to live holy righteous lives, set apart for His purposes. The second kind of obedience is specific obedience; to specific callings and missions that God gives us. For example, our work in Africa is a specific call to obedience for Ali and I.

Can we be obedient in the general things and not in the specific things, or vice versa? I don't think we can. Out of our love for God, obedience should be our natural instinct, our default. We cannot pick and choose. There is no excuse, the sacrifices we seemingly make for God cannot justify our disobedience.

2 John v 5-6 reads,

> ... *"I am not writing you a new command but one we have had from the beginning. I ask that we love one another. And this is love: that we walk in obedience to His commands. As you have heard from the beginning, His command is that you walk in love".*

1 John 3 v 21-24 reads,

> *"Dear friends, if our hearts do not condemn us, we have confidence before God and receive from Him anything we ask, because we keep his commands and do what pleases Him. And this is His command: to believe in the name of His Son, Jesus Christ, and to love one another as He commanded us. The one who keeps God's commands lives in Him, and He in them".*

I understand it is not always easy. If you know there is an area of disobedience in your life, then do something about it. Pray, sit down with Him, and talk to Him about it, speak to someone else who you trust, ask someone to pray. Dont ignore it. With God there is always a way back through repentance. Jesus could return at any moment, be obedient and be ready. Obedience is better than sacrifice.

All we are and all we need is found in the person of Jesus Christ. When we know who we are in Him, when we fully understand it, when we acknowledge it, accept it and live our lives in obedience to Him, our lives will be totally transformed. Our posture will change, and we will, at last, live the full life that is promised us in John 10:10. Generally, this transformation does not happen overnight, it is a journey. So that means we have to participate in it. We have a part to play, working in partnership with Holy Spirit. We need to get on with it, time is short. No longer do we have time to waste. Be obedient, do the things He is telling you to do. Do it today, don't delay a minute longer.

Obedience is part of our journey to spiritual maturity.

'Enter In'

Will you be ready to stand for Christ?

Jesus is coming back very soon for His Bride the Church, and we need to be ready for His return. Those who are not ready may be left behind on the earth. It will then be very difficult to receive eternal salvation. Don't leave it too long, Jesus is going to come back whether you are ready or not. He is coming soon. If you're not ready, He may not recognise you. Life on earth after that day will be very difficult. Don't be one of those who He does not recognise, don't be left behind.

Jesus has already done everything necessary on the cross. He has given you all that you need to be ready. He gave it freely as a gift, you received salvation at no cost to yourself. Because of God's grace Jesus paid the price. You now have everything within you that you need to live a life holy and set apart for God's purposes. The power within you by His Spirit, which you received on the day you accepted Him, cannot be taken away from you. You must now live and work in partnership with His Spirit to live the life He has called you to and be ready on the day He returns for his Bride. You should work out your journey of salvation day by day, living a life of repentance. Please hear me here, I am not talking about a salvation of works, where you must do good works in order to receive salvation. You have already received everything you need the day you accepted

Jesus, but you must choose each day to 'out work' your salvation with fear and trembling.

God sees your heart; is your heart circumcised? Is it a clean and pure vessel, are you living a righteous life? Is your life holy and set apart for God's purposes? Are you living for Him every day?

Ambassadors of God, living on earth as if we are in heaven

We are now in a new era, we are in the end-of-the-end days and life is getting harder. It is getting more and more difficult to live an authentic Christian life, to live and speak biblical truth. It is going to get much harder. For us to survive the days that lie ahead we need to be sure of who we are in Christ Jesus. We need to be free of all fear and we need to be living as if we are already in heaven. What do I mean by this? Let us remember that we are eternal beings. The unsaved are also eternal beings. The saved are saved to an eternity with God, in heaven; the lost are lost to an eternity absent from God, in hell.

As Christians we are God's ambassadors on this Earth. We are eternal, heavenly souls living on this earth in earthly human bodies. We have a mission here on Earth as ambassadors of God. An ambassador is the highest-ranking representative of a country, resident in a host country. Ambassadors are diplomats, they conduct official negotiations and maintain relations between the two countries. The ambassador speaks on behalf of the Sovereign. They are tactful and skilful in managing delicate situations and in handling people. The host country usually allows the ambassador control of specific territory, 'the embassy', and they are given diplomatic immunity in the host country.

What does this look like for us as Christians, God's ambassadors on earth? What is our role here as we speak on behalf of our Sovereign, King Jesus? You could say we are aliens; we are not of this earth; we are from another place. We belong to heaven, but we reside here on earth for a time, to do a job. We are on a mission. We also have immunity, though our immunity is not granted by Earth but by Heaven. We are covered and protected by God. We are healed and cleansed by the blood of Jesus.

Our mission is the great commission; we are to go out into the highways and the byways to reach the least and the lost for Jesus, to make disciples. We must tell the story of Jesus and speak of why He came and what He did; what it means to us and what it means to those who don't yet know Him. Time is short, there are many people who are going to live out their eternity in hell; we have a responsibility. We have work to do. It's time to get real, it's time to step outside of the safety and security of our church buildings. It's a time of breakout, the church walls must come down. We have been restricted and contained for far too long. It's time for us to operate in the unique callings, giftings and challenges that God has given us. We are each unique but also universal in the Body of Christ. We are to stand as individuals, but we are also to be part of the larger Christian body of believers, standing together and fighting for each other.

It is getting harder and harder in these end days to speak the truth and we need, more than ever before, to be grounded in scripture. Our hearts need to be beating as one with His heart; we need to know His heart and His mind, and we need to be able to communicate that to others. If we are not strong in our faith we will give up on our mission. Many have already done so. Have you given up? Have you decided that life is easier without Jesus, that it is easier to agree with the world's values and morals than to put your neck on the line and speak up for the truths of the Bible?

What does it mean for us to live our lives as if we are already in heaven?

We need to be living in this World, but we need to be separate from it at the same time. We need to have our feet on the earth physically and to be sharing life with the least and the lost physically, but our spirits need to be soaring in the heavenly places. We need to be thinking as God thinks, seeing as He sees and operating in the way that He operates. We are His hands and feet on earth, and we need to be sure that our lives emulate Him here. We must stop thinking and operating out of our fleshly beings and start to think and operate as the heavenly beings that we really are. We must be different. It is no longer acceptable for us to do what we want to do; we should only ever do what He wants us to do. We should mirror heaven here on earth. Our life and our character, our actions and our words, should reflect heaven on this earth. Ephesians 2:6 says,

"And God raised us up with Christ and seated us with him in the heavenly realms in Christ Jesus,"

We are seated in heavenly places with Christ Jesus. This is what scripture tells us, and we need to learn to operate our earthly life from that heavenly place.

This heavenly life really is available to us right now!

Don't be downtrodden, don't be beaten; stand up and fight back. Remember that this life I am talking about really is possible. As I said earlier, we have the Spirit of the Living God residing within our souls, the same Spirit that raised Jesus from the dead. It is possible for us to live holy lives set apart for His purposes. We are being sanctified, made holy, mirroring Christ, each day becoming more like Jesus, being changed from one degree of glory to another.

Come on, let's do this, lets fight back. We need to die, and then we can live the remaining time we have on this earth from our place, seated with Christ in the heavenly realm. Let's make the time we have left count; let Jesus recognise us as He comes back on the clouds for His Bride. Don't be left behind, let us rise up with Him on that great and glorious day.

We must live now on earth as if we are in heaven.

How will He recognise us?

As we are living our sanctified lives and as we grow day by day to be more like Jesus, the light within us increases and the darkness within us decreases. We need to be full of light.

A few months ago, I was having my quiet time with the Lord. I sensed my inner being was full of light, though I was aware of patches of darkness within me too. A few days later I woke up in the morning and, as I awoke, I became conscious of an experience I was having. I was pulling strings of darkness out from within myself, and saying I needed to get rid of all this darkness; it all needs to go. I told my husband about this, and He reminded me of the time a few days earlier during my quiet time when I had sensed the darkness within me.

I know that God is wanting us to be full of light. He wants us radiating His light wherever we go. Darkness cannot be hidden in light, and we need to be light givers. We need to carry our light into the darkness of the world we live in. I believe that it is the light that Jesus will recognise within our spirits on that day. At that moment, in an instant, the sanctification process will be complete, we will be made totally and completely holy, we will be totally consumed in light and all the darkness will be gone in an instant. In that moment we will rise to meet Him in the air.

In order for Jesus to recognise us we need to be walking in light; working out our salvation; walking on that road of sanctification; being changed from one degree of glory to another; becoming more like Jesus' day by day. If we are on that journey He will recognise us, and the work will be completed in that instant. We will be saved.

Are you ready?

This is an important question. Please, I beg you, take it seriously, check your hearts right now. Jesus is coming back very soon. None of us knows the day or the hour, but we should recognise the season. We are in that season. Be assured, Jesus could return at any moment - a day, a week, a year, 5 years, 10 years. No one knows, only God the Father; Jesus himself does not know. Mark 13:32 tells us this,

> *"But about that day or hour no one knows, not even the angels in heaven, nor the Son, but only the Father."*

Even if you have prayed a salvation prayer you could be left behind if you are not ready. Remember you were given all you need on that day of your salvation, don't waste it. Make it count. Jesus died so that you could be saved. Think carefully about the consequences of making ungodly choices and living your life for yourself rather than for Jesus. He gave His life for you. Are you prepared to give your life for Him? None of us are perfect, that will come when we meet Jesus. Until then, we are to live our lives honouring Him and working out our salvation. We are to work in partnership with Holy Spirit and be prepared to deal with issues in us as they arise, as we are made aware of them. If we are on this journey and if our hearts are such that we are yearning each day to be more like Jesus, if we are willing to deal with our stuff and are not deliberately ignoring the things Holy Spirit is revealing to us, we will be saved. Let us keep on this journey with Jesus until He returns for us. He is coming soon.

It is time to 'Enter In'

On Monday, 4th May 2020, I was having my time with Jesus and decided to take a break. I went downstairs and decided to do some painting. I am not an artist and have painted only three things in my life; I can't even call them pictures. Due to COVID our daughter was staying with us, she is very artistic. She had her paints on the shelf in the dining room and I thought I would give it a go. I had no idea what I wanted to paint so I started by painting a flower which was a disaster. I was not put off and felt like I needed to continue, so I started again and painted a cross. I then added red for spots of blood, and then a crown of thorns. Next I wanted to drape a purple cloth over the cross, though it didn't really drape. I added some yellow and began to think about the veil in the temple. I added my representation of the veil, and this is what I ended up with:

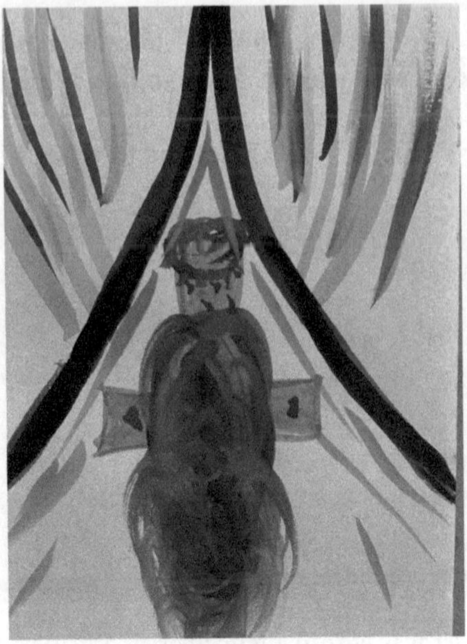

To you, I am sure it does not look like anything, but as I looked at it, to me it was more than just a painting. I felt like the Lord wanted to speak to me through it. So, I started to pray.

I called this painting, "Enter In".

Let me talk for a minute about the veil and entering into the Holy of Holies. When Jesus died on the cross something incredible took place. The veil in the Temple was torn in two, it was ripped from the top to the bottom, and this opened the way in to the Holy of Holies, which was the presence of God.

Matthew 27:51 reads,

> *"At that moment the curtain of the temple was torn in two from top to bottom. The earth shook, the rocks split."*

Let me explain the significance of this.

When Moses was instructed by God to build the tabernacle, the instructions were very precise. You can find these instructions in Exodus 25-31. There were three sections to the structure. There was the Outer Court, the Holy Place and the Holy of Holies.

The Outer Court was within a fenced area, outside a tent structure. The tent structure was the Holy Place and within the Holy Place was the Holy of Holies which was separated by a veil or a curtain. The Holy of Holies could only be entered once a year by the High Priest on the Day of Atonement when he was to enter in and sprinkle the blood of sacrificed animals. A bull was offered as atonement, or compensation for the Priest and his household, and a goat was offered as atonement for the people. If the High Priest did not prepare himself properly, and did not offer the correct sacrifice, or if he entered the Holy of Holies at any other time than the day of

atonement, he would be struck down dead.
No one else could enter behind the veil into the Holy of Holies, into the presence of God, only the High Priest. The veil was a physical, visible barrier indicating that access to God was strictly prohibited because of His holiness. It is very important to remember here that the holiness of God remains unchanged, even after the veil is torn and Jesus has dealt with sin. God is still a holy God, and He cannot tolerate sin.

So, what changed? When Jesus died on the cross, His death provided the appropriate sacrifice, a one and only, for all time, sacrifice, a sacrifice which bulls and goats could not provide.

Hebrews 10:4 says,

> *"It is impossible for the blood of bulls and goats to take away sins".*

So now when we read Matthew 27:51, we can see its significance:

> *"At that moment the curtain of the temple was torn in two from top to bottom, the earth shook, the rocks split."*

Jesus has made a way for us to enter the Holy of Holies and into the Holy presence of God through His death on the cross. Anyone, who accepts Jesus Christ as their Saviour, by acknowledging that they are a sinner, repenting of their sin and asking God for His forgiveness, can now 'Enter In.' God in His mercy and grace has accepted, forgiven, saved, and set them free. He has made a way for them to enter Into the fullness of Christ Jesus. It really is that simple. So why am I telling you all this and what does it have to do with my painting?

When I was praying for God to show me what the painting meant, I felt He was saying that He wanted me to 'Enter In' to a new place, a deeper place, somewhere I had never been before. He wanted me to enter in to the Holy of Holies. Now you might be saying, if you have accepted Jesus then you have already entered into the Holy of Holies. That is true – the curtain has been torn in two, giving us free and full access, to constantly dwell in the glorious presence of the King of kings, in the Holy of Holies. This is a new, fresh and growing revelation for me.

Even though I am in the Holy of Holies, I do not live my life accordingly, I do not live my life as if I am in that place, in His glorious presence 24 hours a day. Life gets in the way, I get in the way. God has so much more for me. In order for me to have and experience more of Him, I must give more of myself.

A friend of mine explained to me that in the Holy of Holies there is no natural light and that light comes through revelation. As we spend time in His presence, seeking more of Him we gain the revelation that is needed for us to be fully present in the moment, in that place. The light comes from within and illuminates the truth and reality of where it is that we dwell, in the Holy of Holies. It is through intimacy with God that these truths are unveiled as revelation brings light. It is not something we can do or decide or earn. It is as we prioritise Him above all else that revelation is released. Luke 1:77-79 gives an example of revelation bringing light as Simeon recognised Jesus, he said "a light of revelation to the nations."

When I read Isaiah's account of the throne room in Isaiah 6 and John's account in Revelation 4, it makes my heart pound, and I desire that kind of revelation. In Isaiah 6:1-8, we read,

> *"In the year that King Uzziah died, I saw the Lord, high and exalted, seated on a throne; and the train of his robe filled the temple. Above him were seraphim, each with six wings: With two wings they covered their faces, with two they covered their feet, and with two they were flying. And they were calling to one another:*

> *"Holy, holy, holy is the Lord Almighty; the whole earth is full of his glory."*
>
> *At the sound of their voices the doorposts and thresholds shook and the temple was filled with smoke. "Woe to me!" I cried. "I am ruined! For I am a man of unclean lips, and I live among a people of unclean lips, and my eyes have seen the King, the Lord Almighty." Then one of the seraphim flew to me with a live coal in his hand, which he had taken with tongs from the altar. With it he touched my mouth and said, "See, this has touched your lips; your guilt is taken away and your sin atoned for." Then I heard the voice of the Lord saying, "Whom shall I send? And who will go for us?" And I said, "Here am I. Send me".*

You can read John's account in Revelation 4:1-11.

I am very aware that these two accounts are speaking of the experiential encounters of two different men with a living God. I am also very aware that it is not the experiences and encounters that we should be chasing after. I believe that if we set our hearts and minds like flint to chase after Him, and Him alone, if we seek His face, if our heart's one and only desire is to know Him more, to fully know Him, then we too will encounter God in new ways. Jesus died so that we could have full access to God and all He holds for us. We have to resolutely seek Him and only Him, laying aside all of our earthly desires in order for us to experience everything that He holds for us. We need to position ourselves, in that secret place, totally abandoned and emptied of everything of us, in order for us to embrace all of Him and all He has for us.

As I have been writing this chapter, I have had incredible revelation. I have been a Christian for nearly 40 years, I have known all these things in my mind, but this last week, for the first time I have had a heart revelation of my position in Christ Jesus. I am in the Holy of Holies and I need to 'Enter In' to that truth and all that it means. I need to start to live my life from that place on a daily basis. I urge you to ask God to give you that same revelation, it is wonderful. Our lives with Christ Jesus are so much more than many of us fully understand. It is time for a greater revelation of who we are in Jesus and who He is in us.

Working out our salvation

The day we are born again is just the beginning, the start of a new and exciting life journey with Jesus. Our walk of faith, our journey of sanctification, has begun. This means that we, as Christians, are now on a daily walk of becoming more and more like Jesus. Paul told the church in Philippi that they were to work out their salvation. Philippians 2:12 says,

> *"Therefore, my dear friends, as you have always obeyed, not only in my presence, but now much more in my absence, continue to work out your salvation with fear and trembling."*

Paul was writing to Christians. He told them to continue. It doesn't end when we are saved, it is just the beginning of a new transformed life. Paul is talking to you and to me. We have to do something. Salvation is not a passive thing that just happens to us, it is a daily walk with Jesus. We live our lives every day wanting to please God by doing what is good and right, because we love Him. We have Holy Spirit within us to help us and guide us along the way.

In my painting, I am one with Christ on the cross, I am in Him and He is in me. The cross is in front of me and, as I was looking at the painting, the words of that song came into my mind:

Christ is Enough, by Hillsong.

> *"The cross before me, the world behind me, no turning back no turning back."*

I was also reminded of a picture I had a few years ago, of a Globe. God's hand was coming out of heaven and grabbing my hand, He was gripping me and I was gripping Him. He was pulling me upwards. I knew that my feet had to be lifted off the earth. I had to be separate from the Earth. He was calling me to be separated unto Himself.

I believe God wants us to 'Enter In' to all He has for us, and we can only do that by 'Entering In' to the full truth of who we are, whose we are and where we are. This often needs greater revelation from Christ, to light up and illuminate this truth in our hearts. He wants us to separate ourselves from the evil of this world and come into a new and glorious place in His presence. Until we have received this revelation, it can be difficult, but once we understand this truth, separating ourselves from the evils of this world becomes more of a priority. We will have no desire to entertain any of the evil that surrounds us.

It is not easy; it is an ongoing process of daily repentance and as we deal with the stuff the world has contaminated us with, as we continue to prepare ourselves by 'Entering In' to the reality of the truth we have received, our desires for the things of this world will become less and less, as we are transformed from one degree of glory to another.

I have had some amazing encounters with God over the years and have felt His presence many times, but I really believe there is so much more. I believe there is another level that I have not reached. I don't believe I have fully 'Entered In' to all that He has for me yet. We have to make a choice, we need to have a desire for more. It is not a passive thing that will just happen, we have to be active in this and much of it is about our intimacy with Jesus. We need to seek Him more than ever before. This will mean we have to make more sacrifices than ever before in order to give Him more of our time. I believe there is an urgency about this, in these end-of-the-end-days.

I believe that God is bringing about a fresh awakening upon the World, and we are at the brink of something incredible. In the painting, I am one with Christ, I am intrinsically a part of Him, and He is a part of me. I am one with His suffering, we are one and we are about to enter into something together as one. We are stood at the entrance. I felt that whatever it was we were entering into would begin around Pentecost 2020.

Could we have the faith to believe that we have now entered a new wave of an amazing outpouring of God's spirit on the Earth, like never seen since the first Pentecost? Could we see a fresh awakening beginning to unfold across the whole world? I believe it has started, and it is different to anything we have experienced before. I know personally it has started for me, I am changed and continue to be changed. Let us not be looking for how it was in the past, the first Pentecost or the revivals of years gone by. Let's not be looking for the second Toronto blessing. This is something new, and if we are looking for how it was before, there is a chance we will miss it. God is a creative God, and this is different to what has gone before. He is doing a new thing, and it has begun. This is a one-on-one awakening; I believe many are being woken up to who God is, and who they are in Him, and to the reality of what that means in these end-of-the-end days. It is quieter, and it is a deep, individual, personal awakening that will last. It is deep, it is pure; it may be painful, but it is necessary if we are to stand. I know it is happening because it is happening to me.

If we choose to be bold, brave and courageous and enter into this new time, this new season, this new era, it will be a place of great sacrifice, but it will also be a place of great blessing. It is a place of fresh anointing, a place of power and authority in the name of Jesus. A new Church era is being birthed, beginning now, as we move out of our confinement and 'Enter In' to all that God is doing.

There will be the extremes of the highs of walking in our power and authority in the name of Jesus, to the lows and many struggles and much pain, that will come with that. We will be mocked, and we will be persecuted. There are most certainly difficult times ahead of us as we move into this new era. The Bible says very clearly that persecution will come, and Christians will suffer. You just need to look at the apostle Paul's life. Our experience of life as the Church is going to look very different than what it did prior to the emergence of this Corona Virus, and, unfortunately, some will fall away and decide it is too hard.

Hebrews 10:38, in The Living Bible (TLB), reads,

> *"And those whose faith has made them good in God's sight must live by faith, trusting him in everything. Otherwise, if they shrink back, God will have no pleasure in them."*

Dr Martyn Lloyd-Jones said:

"There is no grosser or greater misrepresentation of the Christian message than that which depicts it as offering a life of ease with no battle and struggle at all...... Sooner or later every believer discovers that the Christian life is a battleground not a playground."

(The Christian Warfare: An Exposition of Ephesians 6:10–13 (Baker Books, 1998) p.20.)

Let us live by faith and trust Him. Let's not shrink back, as living our life for Christ Jesus becomes more and more difficult as the Day draws near.

I am so excited and feel so privileged to be living in these times. Jesus is coming back very soon. The first Pentecost was the beginning of the work of the Spirit on earth through the Early Church. This second, fresh Pentecost awakening has now begun, as we draw near to the end of the age. A final wave, a last push to see the Church how it was intended to be, just like the Early Church, as it was in

Acts. To see the World saved before the wrath of God is poured out upon the earth. I believe with all my heart that this new era is upon us. Isaiah 43:19 (NLT), reads,

> *"For I am about to do something new. See, I have already begun! Do you not see it? I will make a pathway through the wilderness. I will create rivers in the dry wasteland."*

If you are feeling a little unsettled, or uneasy or struggle with change and things being different, just remember that Jesus is right there with you. Remember, He is one with you and you have Holy Spirit to strengthen you, guide you and encourage you in all that is happening right now. He says to you, "**Do NOT** be afraid".

Isaiah 41:13 says,

> *"For I am the Lord your God who takes hold of your right hand and says to you, "Do not fear; I will help you.""*

Philippians 4:6-7 reads,

> *"Do not be anxious about anything, but in every situation, by prayer and petition, with thanksgiving, present your requests to God. And the peace of God, which transcends all understanding, will guard your hearts and your minds in Christ Jesus."*

It's here, it's now. Are you ready to 'ENTER IN' so that you can stand in this final generation?

The New Emerging Church in this 'New Era'

My husband, Ali and I have been involved in local church leadership for many years. We have also been involved in oversees missions work, first in Romania and, for the past 18 years, in Africa. We have seen many expressions of Church, and had the humble privilege of living in a Christian Community for a year in 2014 - 2015.

Before becoming involved in Christian Community, I had found myself, for a number of years, becoming more and more dissatisfied with the traditional style of congregational worship.

The 12 months Ali and I spent living in Community shaped my thoughts and ideas about "church" like no other experience I have had. That year was by no means the easiest, but it shaped me and gave me a vision, that I believe is God's heart for the Church of the future. During our time in community, we lived and worked with a couple who we would now consider to be very special friends, Roger and Glenys London. They taught us so much and continue to do so. Their teaching and mentorship have been pivotal in the shaping of my Christian walk and ministry over these past few years.

While living in a community setting, I was able to see how it might be, if every person involved was on the same page and working towards the same vision.

After leaving community life we went to live in Sierra Leone, West Africa, for a couple of years. This had been our calling for a long time, since our children were small. I remember, when we first arrived, we were stood in the parlour. I knew in that moment, that we were right in the centre of God's will for our lives at that time; it was a wonderful feeling. After waiting for 15 years for God to take us to that place, it was only to last for two years and then He brought us back to the UK. I was so disappointed and upset that we had to come home, but God had worked in an incredible way. We now have a ministry in Kailahun, Sierra Leone, called Maranatha Christian Outreach Ministries working with local pastors and church leaders. We facilitate them to go out into villages and communities to preach the good news of Jesus and to train and encourage local pastors in discipleship. Many lives are being touched.

When we came back from Africa, we stayed with my parents for around 18 months. During that time, we attended a church we had attended prior to going to Africa. We spent a lot of time seeking the Lord as to where He wanted us and what He wanted us to do. It was a strange season as we were not working. We had no ministry here in the UK and we were just attending church on Sundays. After being so busy for most of our lives and so fully involved in church life or ministry of some kind it was a bizarre time, but it was also a critical time. God was speaking to us about the way forward. We spent a lot of time, fasting and praying, reading scripture, and seeking God. Gradually He started to put His plan into place for the next season of our lives.

We had friends who were living on the coast in Morecambe, at the foot of the Lake District. They were running a ministry called Grace Ministries, which was a charity shop and a drop-in centre for those in need. Ali and I went over to visit and see what the work was all about and instantly knew we had to be involved. It was a version of a vision the Lord had given me many years ago about church having a shop front presence to build community and reach out to people. We started to travel the 30 minutes' drive each

Wednesday to support Grace Ministries. As we continued to seek the Lord about where He wanted us to live it became very evident that we were to move to Morecambe. It wasn't too long after this that our friends' circumstances changed and they were no longer in a position to run Grace Ministries, and we took over the ownership, management and running of the ministry.

In November 2018, we received the keys to our new home - a three story, Victorian mid-terraced house that needed fully renovating. We moved into a partly renovated house in July 2019. God had moved us to Morecambe and given us a ministry that was all about building community.

Once we had decided that God was calling us to move to Morecambe, we started to visit churches to see where The Lord wanted to plant us. We visited a number of local churches and none of them felt the right fit for us.

Over the few years since we returned from Africa, God had been speaking about house church. We had been down to visit Roger and Glenys in Essex. Roger was reading a book by Wolfgang Simons called 'Houses That Changed the World. When I returned home, I ordered the book and it made so much sense to me. Roger had spoken a lot about community over the years and we knew it was Roger and Glenys' heart and it became our heart also. Over the 18 months of seeking God for direction, He started to release a vision for house church into my heart, and the vision and passion for community started to build. I was very excited about it and wrote it all down, and started talking about house church to friends.

When we were looking for a church in Morecambe this was in the back of my mind all the time. After visiting a number of churches to no avail, I said to Ali that maybe we have to start a house church and he agreed with me.

There was one church however that we had not tried, and so we decided to give it a go. We agreed together that if this wasn't the one, we would start a house church in our home. We visited Gateway Church with another couple who were very close friends of ours, Jeremy and Mary. To our utter amazement we loved it. We all came out feeling very excited because we had found our spiritual home in Morecambe. The four of us started attending together.

At the beginning of 2020, COVID struck, and church was closed. Church put a weekly message out on YouTube, and we used WhatsApp to communicate with one another. I spoke at some point to our church leaders about my vision for house church and it was a surprise for me to hear that they had been talking about similar things, and God was speaking to them about community and covenant. I shared my vision and we talked together about it. When our church leaders said they felt that God was directing them to build a community of house churches I felt so blessed by God's faithfulness. God led us to Gateway Church, and he joined our two visions to become one and, in August 2021, Gateway House Church was born.

My Vision for House Church

There are so many reasons why I feel that house church is the Church of the future, the Church that God sees. I believe it is the only way we will be able to build a community of believers who are in true covenant relationship with one another. It is very difficult to do this in a large group. To be in covenant relationship you need to share your lives together. As we move forward in these end-of-the-end days, we are going to need each other like never before. We will need to trust one another, to have each other's backs, to love, support and encourage one another. These relationships can only happen with a few people. Why did Jesus only have 12 disciples? As we build these Christian communities, church will begin to function as Jesus intended, living, working and ministering as community. We are to love our brothers and sisters and support them physically, emotionally, and spiritually, reaching out together to the least and the lost as the Lord places them in our path.

Jesus wants to refine His Body in preparation for His return for His Bride. Christian relationships need to be strong and faithful, loving, and generous, sensitive, honest, open and true. They need to be covenant relationships where agapè love is evident. Many of us still have much work to do regarding the state of our hearts. The Lord is starting to reveal the hidden things of the heart. The time has come to deal, once and for all, with the issues that have been buried deep down. There is coming a time of great deliverance, healing and maturing. This is very difficult to do in a large congregational setting. There needs to be a deeper level of commitment and trust in relationships between Christians; we need to feel safe and secure in these relationships. This will most easily be found in small house church settings.

I believe that this is the only way church will survive in the days to come as we start to see more and more persecution. The time is coming when it will not be possible to meet freely to worship. Churches will be closed, Christians will be outcast. This will happen much sooner than many believe. We need to be together and have each other's backs. We need to prepare now for this persecution of the Church.

Right through the New Testament we can see house church modelled, Christians met in people's homes where they listened to the apostles' teaching. They worshipped and prayed together; they had fellowship and ate together. This was true community that they were modelling. I believe this is how God always intended church to be. It was the best environment for believers to be discipled, for them to receive teaching, for them to be challenged and for them to grow in their faith. I believe with all of my heart that Christian community is the way forward for the Church.

Covenant Relationships

Covenant relationships are key. Much of what Jesus teaches helps us to understand that Christian community is rooted in covenant.

What is Covenant?

We see examples of covenant in both the Old and the New Testaments. A covenant was similar to what we may call a contract or an agreement, a pact, or a promise. A Will could be classed as a covenant. A covenant would establish the basis for the relationship - it would include conditions, promises and the consequences if conditions were not met. A marriage relationship is probably one covenant relationship that we would most relate to.

Below are a couple of biblical covenants we are all familiar with.

Gods Covenant with Noah

Genesis 9: 8 -13 reads,

> *"Then God said to Noah and to his sons with him: "I now establish my covenant with you and with your descendants after you and with every living creature that was with you—the birds, the livestock and all the wild animals, all those that came out of the ark with you—every living creature on earth. I establish my covenant with you: Never again will all life be destroyed by the waters of a flood; never again will there be a flood to destroy the earth." And God said, "This is the sign of the covenant I am making between me and you and every living creature with you, a covenant for all generations to come: I have set my rainbow in the clouds, and it will be the sign of the covenant between me and the earth".*

This is the covenant that God established with Noah after the flood. God promised that He will never again flood the earth, He promised that humanity will be preserved from that day forward. God also created the rainbow at this point and said that it would be a sign of the covenant, to remind us.

Gods Covenant with Abraham

Genesis 12:1-3 says,

> *The LORD had said to Abram, "Go from your country, your people and your father's household to the land I will show you". "I will make you into a great nation, and I will bless you; I will make your name great, and you will be a blessing. I will bless those who bless you, and whoever curses you I will curse; and all peoples on earth will be blessed through you."*

This covenant is the most central to the biblical story. God promised to make Abraham into a great nation, to give him many descendants.

The New Testament Covenant

A New Covenant was foretold in Jeremiah 31:31:

> *"The days are coming," declares the LORD, "when I will make a new covenant with the people of Israel and with the people of Judah."*

And we find it in Luke 22:14-20:

> *" When the hour came, Jesus and his apostles reclined at the table. And he said to them, "I have eagerly desired to eat this Passover with you before I suffer. For I tell you, I will not eat it again until it finds fulfilment in the kingdom of God." After taking the cup, he gave thanks and said, "Take this and divide it among you. For I tell you I will not drink again from the fruit of the vine until the kingdom of God comes." And he took bread,*

> *gave thanks and broke it, and gave it to them, saying, "This is my body given for you; do this in remembrance of me." In the same way, after the supper he took the cup, saying, "This cup is the new covenant in my blood, which is poured out for you."*

This new covenant brings forgiveness of sin, renewal of the heart and an intimate knowledge of God. Jesus' death on the cross was the introduction of this new covenant.

As you can see, covenants are important to God and would not be entered into lightly. In biblical cultures, covenants would be much better understood than they are today, and would be very strong, solid relationships.

An example of a covenant relationship between two biblical characters would be the relationship between Jonathan and David. Read the story of Jonathan and David and pick out the characteristics within their relationship. See what it looked like, how they related to each other and how their lives were connected by this bond.

Community

A community shares life with one another. They help, support, encourage and forgive one another, though always pointing others to Jesus as their ultimate helper. They are reliant on God, accountable to one another, (though ultimately accountable to God), open, honest, and trustworthy; always keeping confidences. They serve one another in sacrificial love. They do not gossip and do not take advantage of one another. Community is as much about giving as it is about receiving. Covenant relationships should be empathic, balanced, compassionate, trusting and, above all, loving. It is also important that those in community do not become reliant on one relationship. Community should point and direct to a relationship that is reliant on God above all else.

I pray that as you have read about community, covenant relationships and house church that Holy Spirit will have ignited something within you that gives you a desire to seek for more. Pray and ask the Lord if you are planted in the right place for this new era. If you are, that's great. I am definately not condoning moving church for the sake of it. What I am saying is that you need to be in the right place for you, as we move into these end-of-the-end days. We need to be in community where we will be loved, supported, challenged, and cherished. But, most of all, a place where we will be made ready for the soon coming of Jesus for His Bride, the Church.

Believe and Belong

One of the key things about modern evangelical churches is that we are encouraged to bring our unsaved friends along to church. They will be made to feel very welcome and to feel like they belong. The hope being that, eventually, they will believe and become a Christian. The problem with this model is that the content of the church service is often adjusted so that visitors are made to feel comfortable and at home. Unfortunately, if someone who is not a believer, feels comfortable when they are in church, church is not fulfilling its purpose. The House of God should be a place of reverence, a place where believers are challenged and changed, moulded, and shaped, remodelled into the people God created them to be. We should not try to make church a comfortable place. Obviously, we should always make people feel welcome, which is very much different to making them feel comfortable.

Many of the large evangelical, charismatic churches are full to the brim of people who love to come and see their friends, sing songs, listen to nice encouraging, uplifting messages and yet still remain unchanged.

I believe church is for disciples of Jesus, just as it was in the days of the Bible. The disciples and believers came together to hear the apostles' teaching and to be community together, to love and care for one another. They were challenged by the apostles' teachings.

I'm sure some were very challenging; you only need to read Paul's letters to see this.

House church is a place where we mature, with God as our Father and our all. We are challenged, we are accountable, we learn and we serve. I believe this is the church Jesus intended, this is the church I see.

We reach people out in the highways and byways; we build friendships and tell them about Jesus. Places like Grace Ministries, our little Charity Shop and Drop-In centre in Morecambe, become small hubs where community is built, and Jesus is shared. Once they understand and come to faith they are then invited to church where their faith will be built up and they will mature into fully fledged disciples of Jesus Christ. Once they believe, they are invited to belong. Not everyone will agree with this model, they will say church should be open to anyone, and it is, but not the Sunday morning meetings. In our church, we have other entry points, Grace Ministries being the main one. We run Alpha Courses there, we have monthly women's and men's morning breakfast meetings, a church walk. Once a month we have a gathered meeting which is open to other churches and to non-believers.

This is a new era, we are living in days where we need to be ready and prepared for what lies ahead, as well as being ready for Jesus' return. It will become more and more difficult for traditional church to gather together as the days grow darker. Let us start to adjust now so we will not be taken by surprise.

The Church will rise up and stand in these end-of-the-end days, but not the Church we have designed, the church God has designed.

A Pink Hoody, an Afternoon Tea, and a Jar of Ghee

In conclusion, I would like to share a little of what the Lord has been doing in my own life during these days. I feel that by sharing some of these small areas of change, it may encourage some who are reading. It is so important that in our journey, our walk with the Lord, that we are aware of ourselves, our vulnerabilities, our weaknesses, as well as our strengths. We also need to be aware of how we are changing from day-to-day.

Many years ago, I was told that it wasn't good to 'navel gaze' and that caused me some issues as I thought that meant I was not to look at myself in any way. God had forgiven me and so I didn't need to look at myself anymore. As the years have gone by and I have grown older and matured in my faith, I now know that maybe that was not the best advice. I have come to realise that it is very important for me to take time to look at and examine myself. This small example shows how we can be so easily influenced by the words of well-meaning people. There are actually many scriptures that talk of self-examination.

For instance, in 2 Corinthians 13:5, we read,

> *"Examine yourselves to see whether you are in the faith; test yourselves. Do you not realize that Christ Jesus is in you unless, of course, you fail the test?"*

The Bible tells us that we should be changing from one degree of glory to another, as in 2 Corinthians 3:18:

> *"And we all, who with unveiled faces contemplate the Lord's glory, are being transformed into his image with ever-increasing glory, which comes from the Lord, who is the Spirit."*

Each day we should become more like Jesus. The longer we journey with Jesus, the more time we spend with Him, the more we should be shaped by Him. With that in mind, it is very important that we look at ourselves and our lives to ensure that each day we look a little more like Jesus. Our lifestyle, our life choices, and our actions should reflect Him. If we don't regularly check ourselves and evaluate ourselves, our lives, and our lifestyle, it is easy for us to miss things. Sin creeps in and we don't even notice! It is so important we spend time in God's presence and ask Holy Spirit to reveal areas of our lives that may need some work.

I am not talking here about working for our salvation, we are saved by grace, and we are clothed with the righteousness of Christ. We just have to remember daily who He is and who we are in Him. We need to operate in the fullness of who we are in Christ Jesus. We need to believe what He says about us and live the lives that He has called us to.

When we went into the COVID lockdown back in March 2020, I painted the picture of 'Entering In'. I felt the Lord was saying that we were in a new era and that it was a 'New Pentecost'. I know, without a doubt, that I have changed as God has been working in my life since then.

I have changed physically, emotionally, and spiritually. I have made some life choice changes because of things I believe the Lord has been saying to me. What is the point of God speaking into our hearts if we are not going to respond to the things He is saying to us or showing us? If we do not walk in obedience and respond to the things He shows us, He may stop speaking to us! Why would He speak if we don't respond to Him? I wouldn't speak to someone who ignored me. The other possibility is that we move away from Him, we move out of ear shot. He is speaking but we are not in a position to listen to what He is saying.

So how have I changed? What things have I changed in my life during this time? What have I done in obedience to the things I believe the Lord has been saying to me?

Time alone with Jesus

The first thing is that I started to spend more time with Jesus. This has always been something I have struggled with throughout my life. Making time to have a quiet time on my own with Him has always been difficult and it still is not easy. I have not mastered it. Lockdown was a great opportunity to do something about this. I have a room which I use as an office and a prayer room, and I started to go in there first thing in the morning to spend time with the Lord. In the past it has been a little sporadic. I have always had good intentions but generally been distracted with one thing or another. I now try to go in there first before anything else happens and, surprise, surprise, the more intentional time I spend with the Lord, the more I hear Him. Don't get me wrong, I have been a Christian for many years and have had different seasons of listening and hearing from God and He can speak anytime if we are open. This, however, has been an intentional time of listening to what He has wanted to say to me at this time. I felt He was calling me to do this, and that He had things He wanted to say to me, things He wanted to show me.

There was so much I started to feel and think about, and mull around in my mind. Much of what I was thinking and feeling, I believe was from the Lord. One day I prayed and asked God what He wanted me to do with the things He was saying to me. As I prayed, I had a real sense that He was saying I should write a book.

That was a real surprise to me, as writing a book has never been on my agenda nor something I have had a desire to do. As I have said before, I cannot say 'no' to God, so I was obedient, and started to write down all the things that were mulling around in my mind. If I am honest, I did think that my book would remain on my laptop, but God had a different idea.

My Physical Being

I felt the Lord saying to me in January 2021 that I should lose weight and get my body physically fit. He was saying that the days that lie ahead will be physically challenging, and I will need to be fit in order to do all that He is going to ask of me.

For the first time in my life the scales had touched 13 stone and I knew I needed to act. I do believe the Lord chooses situations in our lives to illustrate His point. His timing is perfect. He knew that I needed the combination of hitting 13 stone and being in a season where I believed Him to be speaking to me. This combination gave me the motivation I needed to succeed in making a life choice about food and eating that has had positive results for both myself and for Ali, my husband.

I have never dieted before and wasn't sure how to go about it. My daughter told me about an app I could download that would help me to count my calories, and that is what I did. In less than one year, I lost two and a half stone just by counting calories and being more aware of the things I was eating. This had a knock-on effect. For the first time in years, I actually looked in the mirror and liked myself. I started putting on a little make up when I went out and generally making more of an effort with my appearance. I have never been big on makeup and fashion, but I have come to realise that it is important that we feel good about ourselves. A little effort can reap great rewards. It was interesting too, that a few weeks after I started watching my food intake, my husband Ali also joined me. He went on to lose 3 stone. This is a great example of how other people can be encouraged by how we live our lives and how they follow when we set good examples. As Christians we should always be living right, and others will watch and see and, eventually, they will follow. As we are obedient to God and live righteous lives, we are leading the way by shining brightly in the darkness around us.

My Feminine Side

Another thing that was a first for me was wearing pink. It may seem strange to some of you reading, that I should even mention this. Grace Ministries is a great ministry but it is also good for my wardrobe, as I get some great bargains. Recently there was a pink hoody in the shop and a friend of mine picked it up and said that she liked it. I have never worn pink or liked the idea of wearing pink, but when I saw this hoody, something rose inside of me, and I really wanted it! I have had so many compliments about how nice it looks on me and it is now one of my favourite tops. As I shared about my pink hoody with a friend of mine, she said something quite profound. She said that it was as if God was bringing out my feminine side. After that I added nail varnish and perfume to my Christmas list, I haven't worn perfume since I was in my early 20's and I have never really bothered painting my nails, but there is now a new desire within me for these things. I find it very strange, but I believe it is part of what God is doing in me.

I recently started to bake cakes; this is also something I have never done before. A friend had brought a tea loaf round for us, and it looked and tasted so good I asked her for the recipe. I started to make tea loaf, then banana bread, and then bran loaf, all very simple recipes, but something new to me. Like I said, I have never been one for baking and I have never really enjoyed cooking. But things are changing.

I believe God is levelling us out. We are created in the image of God, both male and female. So it doesn't take much to work out that God has the perfect balance of male and female within His makeup. I believe, in these days, that He is levelling out the male and female makeup in each of us as we are being made perfect in His image. This is why those things in me needed to change. God continues with His work in me. He is changing how I feel about myself and how I think about certain things; He is even changing what colours I like and what I enjoy spending my time doing. All of these things are important to God.

God has given me a new enjoyment of cooking just at the time when our church has moved from congregational worship to house church. We now have church in our home, and we eat together each Sunday. We have started an Alpha Course at Grace Ministries and I cook for those doing Alpha. I am finding myself inviting people round for meals because we are wanting to build community. I also cook for family during the week. I have never in my life cooked as much and it is NOT a burden. God has given me what I need for this new season. He is incredible.

My Ministry

Something else God has been doing in me is giving me a heart for my brothers and sisters in Christ, a heart for the Church. I am ashamed to say that I have never really had a lot of time for Christians. I have generally been frustrated when people say with their mouth that they are Christians, but their lives do not line up with the Christian faith. My heart has always been more for the lost, those who have not heard the gospel, the outcasts of society. I have, in the past, become very frustrated with Christians who complain and moan about life and expect their church or church leaders to do everything for them. I have never understood why they don't first go to Jesus for themselves for answers, for healing or anything else that they lack. I often struggled and thought that there were many Christians who felt the Church owed them something because they put a few pounds in the offering basket each week. Recently the Lord has been showing me some of the reasons why there are lots of Christians who live this way. Who live defeated lives, who are definitely not the overcomers they are meant to be.

God has been speaking to me and showing me how the Church, in general, has failed in so many ways. I feel a new desire, even an urgency, to reach out and speak to those who are part of the Church but who do not live the full lives they were called to live; they are not transformed, they are not overcomers. I do believe that some are even deceived into believing they are saved, when the reality is that Jesus does not recognise them. They do all the Christian stuff, and talk the Christian talk, but, in reality, they have not surrendered to Jesus and there has been no life transformation.

Much of what you have read is a result of God changing my heart, and speaking to and working in my life. He has given me a real desire to help Christians rediscover who they are in Him, who He is in them and what He is calling them to do in these end-of-the-end days. What He is doing in me I believe He desires to do in others.

My Behaviour

Another thing I felt the Lord doing in me was showing areas of my character and behaviour that were not edifying Him. The first of these things was watching soap operas. I have always watched East Enders, Coronation Street and Emmerdale; I even remember watching Crossroads when that was on years ago. I stopped watching East Enders a while ago, but, recently, I felt the Lord saying I should stop watching soaps altogether. The main reason was because of how much time I was wasting sitting in front of the television as well as the ungodly, worldly story lines. I was complaining that I didn't have enough time to spend with the Lord but was wasting time watching TV. Since then, I have also stopped watching other television programmes that have ungodly content. I have never been able to watch programmes with a lot of bad language and sex scenes, but I enjoyed watching action films and dramas. More recently, I struggle to watch programmes with a lot of violence too. I tend to look now for Netflix series that are PG rated or sometimes a 12. There are some great ones out there.

The Lord also recently showed me that I was controlling. He showed me three different ways in which I attempted to control people, situations, and my own life.

Below is an excerpt from my journal dated 8th September 2021:

> *"Giving up control and allowing God to pilot the plane, in order for me to be released to soar like an eagle. The transformation of a 54-year-old from control to total surrender to Jesus. Those days of dread will disappear for ever when I no longer need to be in control, when I no longer need all the answers. I need to trust God like never before in the days ahead. Part of my refining and purifying is to give up the wanting and needing to be in control".*

Over a period of two or three days, God started to show me the three areas in my life where I felt like I needed to be in control, and I knew He wanted me to deal with these things.

The first was the need for me to control other people

I was in Grace ministries one day and talking to a friend who was working with me. She was having a conversation with one of our 'drop-in' guests. As I was listening to this conversation, I didn't agree with some of what she was saying, so I gave her "a look" as if to say "Be quiet"! A short while later my friend challenged me, and said, "Lorraine, you cannot control what I say." The Lord convicted me in that moment and I apologised and repented. I am now working on this area of my life.

The second was my need to control my own life

We were in a lady's church meeting at my home, discussing Grace Ministries and a Saturday afternoon tea event that we had been talking about organising. I was desperate to get dates in my diary, and to plan it and organise it, but I couldn't get any of the ladies to agree. Someone asked why it had to be planned that way, so structured; we could do it on different days as and when we choose. Again, I was really challenged by the Lord, in that moment, that my life is too structured, planned and organised, and that I need to be a little less rigid, allowing Him to do more of the organising. I needed to loosen off on the control and leave some space for God to work.

The third area was in relation to practical things

For many years now I have felt we need to be prepared practically as the end days come upon us, and one of those ways is to store non-perishable foods. I was making a list of food that we might store and I was researching about butter. I read that ghee was a good alternative with a long shelf life. I then started to think about how many jars I should buy, when I should buy them, and when I should start to store this food. I was getting myself in a real tizz trying to work it all out in my head when, again, I felt God challenge me, about controlling the situations that life lays before me. I must trust Him more and have more faith to believe that, at the appointed time, I will know what I need to do. God will show me all these details without me needing to plan each detail myself. I just need to be aware that this is something I should look at doing and trust Him that, at the appointed time, I will know and understand all the more intricate details necessary. God will give me the right revelation at the right time.

The Lord has shown me that, if I need to be in control all the time, I don't truly trust Him. Day by day I am learning to trust Him more, I am relinquishing control of many areas of my life, and I am starting to see the benefits. I feel so much more at peace as I learn to trust my Heavenly Father in every area of my life, more and more each day. I feel so much freer than before.

The Lord has even healed some areas of my marriage that have been issues for many years, He really is working amazing miracles in these days.

I hope that by me sharing some of the things the Lord has been doing in my life, that it may help you to look at yourself and recognise when God is at work. I believe God has a work to do in every one of us, but we need to be willing to engage with Him and to walk in obedience to the things He is saying. Obedience is definitely a key in us moving deeper and higher with Jesus.

As we obey God, He is pleased with us. The more we obey we find that our faith grows, we see the faithfulness of God in action, and, day by day, we become more like Jesus. We are changed from one degree of glory to another.

God sees our hearts, He loves us so much, He only wants the best for us and only asks us to do things that are good. He is a good God. If we desire to go deeper and higher with Him, we will need to make sacrifices. If however, we choose to live nominal Christian lives, we will miss out on so many good and exciting things that He has for us, we will not live in the fullness of Christ, and our life will not be the best life. We have to trust Him and believe that He really does want the best for us.

Let us remember also that God still loves us, even when we mess up, and that there is always a way back through repentance.

Will you choose to stand and take your place?

God will not ask you to do anything He is not going to equip you for. You have everything you need in Christ. You just need to trust and obey and do the things He calls you to do.

As I bring these ruminations of mine to a close, I am reminded of the old song, 'Trust and obey, for there's no other way, to be happy in Jesus and to trust and obey.'

When we walk with the Lord in the light of His Word,
What a glory He sheds on our way!
While we do His good will, He abides with us still,
And with all who will trust and obey.
Trust and obey, for there's no other way
To be happy in Jesus, but to trust and obey.
Not a shadow can rise, not a cloud in the skies,
But His smile quickly drives it away;
Not a doubt or a fear, not a sigh or a tear,
Can abide while we trust and obey.
Trust and obey, for there's no other way
To be happy in Jesus, but to trust and obey.
Then in fellowship sweet we will sit at His feet.
Or we'll walk by His side in the way.
What He says we will do, where He sends, we will go;
Never fear, only trust and obey.
Trust and obey, for there's no other way
To be happy in Jesus, but to trust and obey.
Oh, Trust and obey, for there's no other way
To be happy in Jesus, but to trust and obey.
And 'Tis so sweet to trust in Jesus,
Just to take Him at His Word;
Just to rest upon His promise,
Just to know, "Thus saith the Lord!"
Jesus, Jesus, how I trust Him!
How I've proved Him o'er and o'er;
Jesus, Jesus, precious Jesus!
Oh, for grace to trust Him more!
Oh, for grace to trust You more!

John H. Sammis (1887)

This is the best way I can end my writing. It is my hope that you will read these lyrics and they will inspire you to live your life accordingly.

As you walk through these days with Jesus in the centre, as you seek His face and position yourself to receive the fullness of all He has for you, I pray that the Lord will bless you and keep you, that the Lord will make His face to shine upon you, that He will be gracious to you and give you peace.

Peace is key here; I hope and pray that these writings have encouraged you and spurred you on to seek His face like never before. I pray you will be prepared to lay your heart on the altar, to listen, respond, and allow Him to change, heal, refine and remould you. He has a plan and a purpose for your future and a great and vital role for you to play.

Will you choose to stand in this final generation and enter in to all that is available to you, all that He has for you as we march forward together as warriors in these end-of-the-end days? Be READY, Jesus is coming back for His Bride very soon. He is waking His Church up. It is a time of vital preparation. Be ready for the days that lie ahead and be ready for the return of Jesus as He comes for His Bride, the Church.

Stand Up and Enter In.

MARANATHA – Come Lord Jesus.

Appendix

Britt Gillette is the founder of End Times Bible Prophecy, a website dedicated to helping people better understand biblical prophecy.

In this issue of the End Times Bible Prophecy newsletter, we discuss how close we may be to the Tribulation...

Are We on the Verge of the Tribulation?

"For the essence of prophecy is to give a clear witness for Jesus." ***Revelation 19:10*** (NLT)

After two years of global turmoil, people are starting to realize we aren't going to "return to normal." We've endured a global pandemic, widespread social unrest, vaccine passports, and compounding global supply chain issues. Now, we have a major war in Eastern Europe, fuel and food price inflation, and rumours of an impending global financial crisis. Everywhere you look, it seems as though the end is near. Is it? What does the Bible say? How close are the end times, the Tribulation, and the rapture of the church?

Fortunately, we don't have to guess. Jesus Himself told us how to recognize the general timeframe of His return. When the disciples said, "Tell us the signs of your coming and the end of the age" ***(Matthew 24:3)***, Jesus told them a number of things to look for. He then said, "When you see ***all these things***, you can know my return is near. I'm right at the door" ***(Matthew 24:33)***. He also said, "When ***all these things*** begin to happen, look up for your salvation is near!" ***(Luke 21:28)***.

This means the #1 indication Jesus will return soon is all the signs appearing together. Both Jesus and the prophets told us what those signs are, and the appearance of just one is reason enough to take notice. But the arrival of one sign after another demands your attention. It's ***the*** sign Jesus said to look for. This convergence of signs is confirmation our generation will witness the Second Coming – not according to me, but according to Jesus.

The Convergence of Signs

So what are these signs? This article will only cite a few. These signs are undeniable, and their convergence should convince you the return of the Lord is close at hand. They include:

Israel Back in the Land – God promised to bring the Jewish people back into the land of Israel before He returned ***(Jeremiah 23:7-8)***. He said He would call them from "among the nations" (Ezekiel 39:28), from "the farthest corners of the earth" ***(Isaiah 11:12)***, and from "north, south, east, and west" ***(Psalm 107:3)***. He promised to welcome them home from the lands where they were scattered ***(Ezekiel 20:34)***. When they did, He promised to return and establish His everlasting kingdom ***(Isaiah 11:11-12)***.

The Jewish People in Control of Jerusalem – Jesus said armies would surround Jerusalem, destroy the city, and enslave its citizens. The Roman legions fulfilled this prophecy in A.D. 70. Jesus then said people other than the Jewish people will control

Jerusalem for a time, until the Jewish people once again control Jerusalem. When they did, Jesus promised to return **(Luke 21:24-28)**. Since 1967, the Jewish people have controlled Jerusalem.

The Gospel Preached Throughout the World – When asked about the end of the age and the signs of His coming, Jesus said to look for a very specific sign. He said the Gospel will be preached throughout the entire world. Every nation will hear it. And then? And then, the end will come ***(Matthew 24:14)***. For centuries after the crucifixion, the Gospel was confined to a small area surrounding the Mediterranean Sea. In the past two centuries,

Christians have brought the Gospel to every nation in the world. Today, missionaries are in every nation. The Bible is translated in hundreds of languages, and the message of Jesus is sent around the world by radio, TV, satellite, and the Internet. For the first time in history, this generation is on the verge of spreading the Gospel to every last person on earth.

An Increase in Travel and Knowledge – Six hundred years before Jesus, an angel gave Daniel a special message. He said "travel and knowledge" will increase in the end times ***(Daniel 12:4)***. For centuries of human history, dramatic gains in travel and knowledge did NOT take place. Yet the last two hundred years have seen explosions in the speed and frequency of travel as well as the amount and availability of knowledge.

Arrival of the Exponential Curve – Jesus said a variety of global signs will come before His return and the end of the age. These signs will be spiritual, natural, societal, and political in nature. He said they will appear in a distinct way – "like birth pains" (Matthew 24:3-8). This means the frequency and intensity of these signs will increase as we near His return. Our generation has seen the exponential increase in war and famine Jesus said to look for. In the 20th Century alone, more people died from war and famine than lived on the earth when Jesus spoke these words.

Israel Surrounded by Enemies – The Bible says enemies will surround Israel in the end times. Those enemies will say "Come, let us wipe away the nation of Israel. Let's destroy the memory of its existence" ***(Psalm 83:4)*** and "Let us take for ourselves these pasturelands of God" ***(Psalm 83:12)***. Ezekiel said Israel's neighbors will say "God has given their land to us" ***(Ezekiel 11:14-17)***, and "Israel and Judah are ours. We will take possession of them. What do we care if their God is there?" ***(Ezekiel 35:10)***. Ever since the rebirth of Israel in 1948, the daily headlines have included these Bible verses. Israel's Muslim neighbors claim the land of Israel for themselves, and they have no regard for the God of Israel.

Israel's Exceedingly Great Army – Ezekiel said, in the end times, Israel will field "an exceedingly great army" ***(Ezekiel 37:10)***. Zechariah said Israel will be like a fire among sheaves of grain, burning up the neighboring nations ***(Zechariah 12:6)*** and even the weakest Israeli soldier will be like David ***(Zechariah 12:8)***. Since 1948, Israel has fought no less than four conventional wars against its neighbors. Despite being outnumbered more than 50 to 1, Israel has achieved overwhelming victory every time.

Rise of the Gog of Magog Alliance – The Bible says a military alliance that includes Russia, Iran, Turkey, and a number of Muslim nations will attack Israel "in the latter days" ***(Ezekiel 38:8)*** when God brings His people home from among the enemy nations ***(Ezekiel 39:27)***. Today, we see those very nations coming together for the first time – an alliance that has never existed in world history.

Rise of a United Europe – The Bible says a revived Roman Empire will come to power in the end times ***(Daniel 2, Daniel 7, Revelation 17)***. According to Daniel, it will be a ten nation alliance of weak and strong nations. Some parts will be as strong as iron, while other parts will be as weak as clay ***(Daniel 2:42)***. We see the beginning of this alliance in the European Union – a coalition of weak and strong nations struggling to stay together.

The Rise of Global Government – The Bible says a single government will rule the world politically ***(Revelation 13:7)***, religiously ***(Revelation 13:8)***, and economically ***(Revelation 13:16-17)*** in the last days. It will rule over "all people, tribes, and languages" on the face of the earth ***(Revelation 13:7)***. Its authority will be so complete no one will be able to buy or sell anything without its permission ***(Revelation 13:16-17)***. For centuries, a true global government was impossible. Today, world leaders openly discuss it.

Denial of the Signs – Almost two thousand years ago, Peter issued a warning. He said in the last days people will mock the idea of

Jesus returning. They will make fun of those who believe in the Second Coming and say exactly what we hear today – things like, "I thought Jesus was coming back? What happened to His promise? Generation after generation has said He's coming. Yet, since the beginning of the world, everything has remained the same!" ***(2 Peter 3:3-4).***

The Hour is Late

Keep in mind, these signs haven't always been present. Generations of Christians lived and died without witnessing **any** of these signs. For centuries of Christian history, none of these signs were present. Today, they all are. Jesus said when you see these signs, you can know His return is near. He's right at the door ***(Matthew 24:33).*** In fact, Jesus said the generation witnessing these signs will not pass away before He returns ***(Matthew 24:34).*** So despite the skeptics and naysayers, Jesus is coming, and ours is the generation that will witness His return. The convergence of all these signs confirm it.

Are We on the Verge of the Tribulation?

For many years now, we've seen the convergence of the signs Jesus and the prophets said to look for. Now, in 2022, we see a specific alignment of events that could lead to the outbreak of the Tribulation at any moment. These specific events are identical in nature to the events the Bible says will occur during the Tribulation. Whether or not these events are merely a preview of the events to come, or the actual events the Bible describes for the Tribulation, remains to be seen. However, keep in mind these events will roll out in the midst of the very season when Jesus said He would return.

So what are these possible Tribulation events in the making? Here are just a few:

Central Bank Digital Currencies – Over the past couple of years, central banks have openly discussed the introduction Central Bank Digital Currencies (CBDCs). The central banks wield power over some of the largest economies in the world – the United Kingdom, Canada, China, the European Union, and the United States. Despite these public discussions, conventional wisdom says the rollout of CBDCs remains years in the future. The conventional wisdom is wrong. China has already released a digital yuan, and recently released digital yuan wallets for both Android and iOS smartphones.

In March, President Biden signed an Executive Order titled "Ensuring Responsible Development of Digital Assets." The order requires federal agencies to submit to the President ***within 180 days:***

"a technical evaluation of the technological infrastructure, capacity, and expertise that would be necessary at relevant agencies to facilitate and support the introduction of a CBDC system **should one be proposed**. The evaluation should specifically address the technical risks of the various designs, including with respect to emerging and future technological developments, such as quantum computing."

By September 2022, this technical evaluation will be complete. Then, have no doubt about it – once the next crisis hits, the U.S. will roll out its own CBDC to replace the dollar.

Why does this matter? CBDCs will be centralized, government-controlled programmable currency. This means if the government decides it doesn't like you ***for whatever reason*** (think Canadian truckers), they can cut off your access. In other words, you won't be able to buy or sell. Sound familiar? The Bible says the Antichrist will implement this same system. Those who refuse the mark of the beast will be unable to buy or sell ***(Revelation 13:17)***. We're now on the verge of a global rollout of a technology ***identical in ability*** to the mark of the beast technology the Bible says will dominate the world during the Tribulation.

World War III – The Bible says there will be a World War III **(Revelation 6:4)**, and we're much closer to it today than when 2022 started and probably the closest we've been since the Cuban Missile Crisis in 1962. Every day seems to bring a new escalation between NATO and its allies and Russia over the latter's invasion of Ukraine. NATO has sanctioned Russia, is providing arms to the Ukrainian resistance, and many of its members have called for direct intervention in Ukraine. Even if NATO avoids a direct military conflict, all it takes is for Russia to make one mistake which leads to a deadly strike in Poland, Slovakia, Hungary, or Romania (all NATO members bordering Ukraine), and all of NATO will be obligated to respond. A full-blown war between Russia and NATO means World War III and the likely use of nuclear weapons. In 2019, the U.S. ran a war game to simulate what would happen in the event of a Russian invasion of Ukraine. The result was nuclear war with over a billion people dead. It's a stark reminder that, at any moment, the war in Ukraine could escalate into World War III.

Hyperinflation – In 2022, inflation has become a serious problem for almost every major economy in the world. The March 2022 headline inflation number for the U.S. was 8.5% – the highest since 1981. For the EuroZone, it came in at 7.5%. In Germany, wholesale prices rose 22.6% year-over-year. EU natural gas prices increased six-fold. Global oil prices rose 67%, wheat prices doubled, and corn prices went up 50%. Fuel and food riots have erupted in Peru, Sri Lanka, and Pakistan. And unrest is brewing in countless other countries as well.

Could we be on the brink of hyperinflation? Maybe. Maybe not. But the Bible says the whole world will one day experience hyperinflation. When that happens, an entire day's wages will only buy enough food to barely survive ***(Revelation 6:6).***

Global Famine – As we entered 2022, the world already faced a major food crisis, both in terms of supply and price. Since then, the situation has only gotten worse. The Russian invasion of Ukraine cut off Russian and Ukrainian exports via the Black Sea. Together, they account for 12% of all global calories consumed. The sanctions against Russia have compounded ongoing supply chain issues, and many countries have banned agricultural exports. Add in poor harvests, rampant fertilizer shortages, and an avian flu plague destroying millions of chickens and turkeys, and it becomes clear we're heading toward the worst food crisis in modern times. In fact, it's worse than that. Famine is coming on a mass scale. We simply aren't going to grow enough food in 2022. The result will be a biblical famine. The only question is whether it will be one of the famines Jesus spoke about in Matthew 24:7 or the Tribulation famine of Revelation 6:5-8.

Jesus is Coming Soon

If the world stage is now set for the Tribulation, how close must the rapture be? The Bible says the rapture will take place before the Tribulation. Jesus promised His church, "I will keep you from the hour of trial that is going to come upon the whole world to test the inhabitants of the earth" ***(Revelation 3:10).*** If you're reading this and you're a Christian, your time on this earth is short. Your race ***(1 Corinthians 9:24-27)*** is nearing its end, so make sure to finish well. Live a holy, godly life as you look forward to the day of His coming (2 Peter 3:11-12). Take advantage of every opportunity to spread the Gospel. Go and make disciples of all nations, baptizing them in the name of the Father and of the Son and of the Holy Spirit, and teaching them to obey everything Jesus has commanded ***(Matthew 28:19-20).*** The day will come when you will lose the opportunity to share the Good News of Jesus Christ. So do it now while you still can. Jesus is coming soon.

References

document.desiringgod.org/the-veil-was-torn-in-two-en.pdf

Holy of Holies - Wikipedia

James Smith and Robert Lee in Handfuls on Purpose for Christian Workers and Bible Students (Grand Rapids, Michigan: William B. Eerdmans Publishing Company, 1971. Vol. 8, p.11.)

Strong's concordance says this, Definition 'Leb': "inner man", "mind", "will", "heart" 'Lebab': "heart" (the most interior organ), "being", "think in themselves", "breast", "comfortably", "courage", "midst", "mind", "unawares", "understanding"

The Collins Dictionary definition is this - * A strong or unshakeable belief in something, especially without proof or evidence. * A conviction of the truth of certain doctrines of religion, especially when this is not based on reason. * Complete confidence or trust in a person. P19

HTTPS://www.thinking7.org/resources/the-tabernacle/

Watchmen International – Spiritual Transformation Training Programme

www.end-times-bible-prophecy.com/
www.raptureready.com/2022/04/20/are-we-on-the-verge-of-the-tribulation-by-britt-gillette/

watchmenforchrist.ning.com/profiles/blogs/the-task-of-the-watchman p59

www.jesuswalk.com/manifesto/11_judging.htm

www.compellingtruth.org/definition-of-faith.html

www.bible.com/reading-plans/17704-bible-in-one-year-2020-with-nicky-gumbel/day/197